The Content-Rich Reading & Writing Workshop

A Time-Saving Approach for Making the Most of Your Literacy Block

Nancy Akhavan

New York • Toronto • London • Auckland • Sydney
Mexico City • New Delhi • Hong Kong • Buenos Aires

In memory of Gwennyth Trice,
for inspiring me to teach and learn my entire life

⤨

Cover design by Jorge J. Namerow

Cover photography: children at computer, © Stockbyte™ (www.stockbyte.com);
students looking at project, student work by Nancy Akhavan

Interior design by Sydney Wright

Acquiring Editor: Lois Bridges

Development Editor: Gloria Pipkin

Production Editor: Sarah Glasscock

Copyeditor: Erich Strom

ISBN-13: 978-0-545-04706-7

ISBN-10: 0-545-04706-4

Copyright © 2008 by Nancy Akhavan

All rights reserved. Published by Scholastic Inc.

Printed in the U.S.A.

1 2 3 4 5 6 7 8 9 10   40   14 13 12 11 10 09 08

Contents

The Knowledge Gap

Why There Is an Urgent Need to Ramp Up Content Instruction

Clear, focused content instruction is the gateway to knowledge that all children need to succeed in school. When we focus on science, social studies, and literary works in our classrooms, children learn facts and information about the world that not only contribute to academic success but also provide a level field for exchanging thoughts and ideas. Excellent content teaching helps children be smart (Hirsch, 2003; McKee & Ogle, 2005; Stahl & Shanahan, 2004). It focuses not only on the gathering of facts but also on the thinking processes a child needs to develop.

Excellent content teaching accomplishes the following:

- Develops knowledge—the construction of schemas, or mental models, that store information in our minds

- Joins fact learning with information processing

- Guides children to negotiate information and evaluate information sources

- Builds disciplinary knowledge—the construction of a mental model of history or science

- Provides instruction in a reading and writing workshop, or a literacy block, that encourages children to work with, think, talk, and write about the content

Content and disciplinary knowledge doesn't grow in isolation. This knowledge develops when children are highly motivated to engage with learning (Fountas & Pinnell, 2006). This happens in effective high-poverty and high-minority classrooms, and it can happen in yours. Imagine being able to save time, get to all subject areas, and ensure student learning. Imagine meeting the pressures of district and state mandates, and fulfilling your desire to prepare all children for the future. Focus on content, reading, writing, and thinking, and you can do this work. Ramp up your content instruction by having students do the following:

- Read trade books, leveled text, and textbooks on specific grade-level topics during the workshop

- Talk about rich content issues, information, and new concepts in a variety of contexts

- Write expository essays, summaries, reports of information, and persuasive essays about the content they have studied

- Learn in a workshop setting

Why Ramp Up Content Instruction?

We cannot wait to integrate content studies into our workshops for three compelling reasons:

1. Although reading scores on the National Assessment of Educational Progress improved for Black, White, and Hispanic students in 2007, only the Black-White gap for fourth graders narrowed in comparison with the 1992 and 2005 gaps. The achievement gap as measured by the NAEP test remains unchanged between white students and minority students since 1992 (Lee, Grigg, & Donahue, 2007; Livingstone & Wirt, 2005; National Center for Education Statistics, 2004).

2. Large numbers of students are not leaving elementary school prepared for middle and high school content classes (Slater, 2004).

3. Children need to be challenged; focusing solely on strategy use during the literacy block isn't rigorous (Brown, 2002; Hirsch 2003, 2006; Vacca, 2002).

Teaching content means making social studies, science, and literary standards the centerpiece of your literacy block in a way that entwines developing knowledge with teaching concrete and applicable reading and writing strategies. This occurs when you teach social studies and science during your reading and writing workshops.

Impossible, you think—but not if you are willing to look at science and social studies from a different angle. By blending content studies with reading and writing instruction, you can build children's knowledge without adding on to your already-too-full teaching day. Many authors and researchers call for children to read nonfiction more often than fiction (Harvey, 1998; Pappas, 2006), but scaffolding to content differs from ensuring that children read nonfiction materials, because it is based on standards and grade-level expectations in content.

Does the American Revolution appear in your social studies standards? Then children would read biographies of Americans who took part in the Revolution. Does cell structure appear in your science standards? Then groups would read nonfiction texts (such as leveled texts) and Internet resources about plant and animal cells during reading workshop. When the focus on strategy instruction to develop reading comprehension and writing aptitude marries the content standards, you have a content-focused workshop.

The Achievement Gap Remains Largely Unchanged

The National Assessment of Educational Progress, which tests student ability in 4th, 8th, and 12th grades across the nation, reported that although the gap between reading scores of White and Black fourth graders decreased in 2007, a 27-point disparity remains, and the gap did not decrease significantly for other ethnic groups or for eighth graders. The 26-point score gap between White and Hispanic students in 2007 was not significantly different from the gaps in 2005 or 1998. (See Figure A.1.) In addition, the 2005 NAEP scores for 12th graders indicate that 43 percent of White students scored at or above proficient, compared with 16 percent of

	1998	2000	2002	2003	2005
Point difference between Black students and White students—4th grade	32	34	30	31	29
Point difference between Hispanic students and White students—4th grade	32	35	28	28	26
Point difference between Black students and White students—8th grade	26	not available	27	28	28
Point difference between Hispanic students and White students—8th grade	27	not available	26	27	25

Figure A.1: Gaps in average NAEP reading scores, 4th and 8th grades

Source: U.S. Department of Education, 2007

Black students, 20 percent of Hispanic students, 36 percent of Pacific Islander students, and 26 percent of Native American students (Grigg, Donahue, & Dion, 2007). (See Figure A.2.)

Large Numbers of Students Are Not Prepared for Future Schooling

There is an urgent need residing in our class-rooms today. Many underprepared and disengaged students drop out in high school, and the dropout rate has remained relatively unchanged since 1992 (U.S. Department of Education [ERS], 2007). Although fourth-grade reading scores on the NAEP rose in 2007, only 33 percent of students across the nation—about one-third of the total—scored at or above the proficient level. The number of students proficient by eighth grade does not increase; in 2007 only 31 percent of the students scored at proficient or above—down from 33 percent in 2002. That leaves about two-thirds of the students poorly prepared for high school content courses (Grigg et al., 2007). Figure A.3 charts this information.

	2005
Average score	35
White students	43
Black students	16
Hispanic students	20
Asian/Pacific Islander	36
American Indian/ Alaska Native	26

Figure A.2: 12th-grade NAEP reading scores 2005: Percentage of students scoring at or above proficient by ethnicity

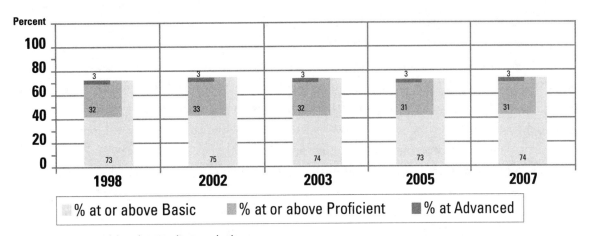

Figure A.3: Eighth-grade NAEP achievement levels

Students need to leave elementary and middle school prepared. We can begin by having students meet grade-level standards. I am not referring to "meeting standards" in the sense that is dictated by high-stakes testing but rather in the sense of developing a whole child, one who knows essential information about the world and can read and write well. I refer to children who "meet standards" as children with every opportunity available to them as they grow, continue to learn, and show what they know on formative classroom assessments. Unfortunately, we have lost sight of this idea of *meeting standards*. Our system has become so clogged with high-stakes accountability testing that we have forgotten about results.

Results should focus on children and should be triumphant. Results mean that children are becoming educated. The numbers in test data are indicators of what children have learned and can do *on a given assessment*. While this doesn't tell us everything a child knows, it is an indicator of a child's ability in relation to a body of knowledge. It is a marker for us to use to know how well prepared children are. When children leave our schools prepared for secondary education, we have results.

Children Need Rigorous Instruction

Rigorous instruction has become a catch-all phrase for *hard*. I don't mean you should throw difficult tasks at children and call your work done. What I intend by using the term *rigorous* is for you to engage children in work and content of substance: work that is interesting, authentic, engaging, and purposeful.

If you think of rigorous instruction as a product of the transmission model of learning, where the teacher and the textbook hold all knowledge and the teacher's job is to transmit the information to her students, I invite you to challenge your thinking. Rigorous instruction doesn't imply the transmission model of teaching. It also doesn't imply that a workshop model, also considered to be a participatory learning model where students construct knowledge, is rigorous just because students interact. Rigorous instruction is content instruction with a balance between learning facts and having opportunities to interact with information to construct mental models, or schemas (VanSledright & Limon, 2006). It is purposeful and engaging for all students. It is the instruction children want and crave. In fact, minority children sometimes tell their teachers and leaders that they want to learn the *real stuff*, the curriculum that mainstream children have access to (Olsen & Jaramillo, 1999). Purposeful, rigorous content instruction takes the following into consideration (Stahl, 2006):

- The facts to be learned

- The development of a mental model to understand the facts

- The learner's previous knowledge and the use of that knowledge to develop a new mental model

Underprepared students are in particular need of purposeful, rigorous instruction. Many diverse, and at-risk students often don't have experiences with the world that mainstream students have and therefore don't share the same mental models. While they have rich mental models about the world, these students need instruction that scaffolds content learning in steps so that they can learn with teacher guidance and then alone (Allington, 2001). Children need to be taught how to remember and how to use what they remember when reading nonfiction, and at-risk children may need additional support.

Traditionally, our secondary schools focus on *assign-and-assess* instruction (Akhavan, 2007). Assign-and-assess instruction is transmission learning. The teacher creates a packet, runs it off, writes the assignment on the whiteboard, gathers the student work and corrects it, assigns a grade, and moves on. There is very little direct instruction given in content areas, and many students need help. They may not have the strategies and skills to learn on their own *and* they may be bored by the transmission learning style (Bransford et al., 2006). At-risk youth need experiences in a safe environment interacting and thinking through content. They need to construct mental models about content (Barton, 2004; Pressley & Wharton-McDonald, 2002).

At-Risk Students Need School to Be Motivating

Children are bored when they do the same thing over and over again. We have become so focused on reading and writing strategies as entities in themselves that we have forgotten about application (Hirsch, 2006; Stahl, 2006). *Using* writing to thoughtfully process new information learned while reading and *learning* interesting facts and information are examples of application. Strategies exist as scaffolds to help our students gain access to content learning and to an equal education. Strategies shouldn't become the be-all and end-all of our daily activities, but this is slowly occurring in our classrooms. After years of focusing on text connections *without* application, our young students are asking us, "*When* do we get to study interesting stuff, teacher?"

Stuff to children is what they find in their books or on the news. It may scroll across the computer screen when they log on. Stuff is what fills the heavy books from current social studies and science adoptions. All of the stuff is important in its own context. It is interesting and engaging, and children need to learn it in order to be educated and to think. To a tween (those kids at that endearing age between 10 and 12) *stuff* is interesting. *Stuff* holds the secret of the universe and *stuff* makes them smart and capable. We know it as content knowledge, domain knowledge, disciplinary knowledge, and vocabulary.

How to Scaffold Content Learning

Scaffolding content learning through effective workshop teaching is the focus of this book. You can also scaffold content learning by using every bit of time available to you. Often, our teaching day is compartmentalized in boxes of time and subject areas—one box of time for language arts (and that is a big box nowadays), one box for math, another for skills. This "box of time" framing leaves little time to teach science and social studies and to meet the needs of struggling readers in the upper-grade classroom.

It is possible to frame time differently. The National Reading Panel recommends that three hours a day be devoted to literacy block (National Institute of Child Health and Human Development [NICHHD], 2000). If this includes direct skills instruction, reading in large and small groups, and writing instruction, there is little time in the day for an ongoing deep, thirsty look at content. You have exactly two-and-a-half hours to do everything else: math, science, social studies, music, art, health, and physical education. Factor in lunch and recess, and time becomes very precious.

To gain time, reframe your thinking and teaching model to squeeze everything into the day without sacrificing reading, writing, or content instruction. Begin your reading or writing workshop with a mini-lesson, followed by a time in class where students read, write, talk, and think about content either alone or together. If you don't prefer a workshop model, think of applying a constructivist learning model to your literacy block. Focus on scaffolding specific instructional points in precise mini-lessons and then follow up with independent work where students have to interact with facts and information rather than regurgitate information in work-sheet packets.

Good Teaching Is an On-Ramp to Learning

Teaching is truly hard work. Finding time in your day for all you have to do can be overwhelming, but in our race to the test-taking finish line, let's not leave the children behind. When you design content-based reading and writing workshops, you open the door for all children to be successful in school. After all, they do need to know information to be educated. Put the children in the context of history and let them relive it. To know something in depth is to understand it. Teach the children how to think like scientists. Teach them the *why* as much as the *what* when they are unlocking the secrets of the world. Teach them to think, teach them facts, teach them well, and you give them an on-ramp to success.

On-Ramp to Learning ▷ **Make Content the Centerpiece of Instruction**

- ◆ Content knowledge is closely associated with reading achievement.
- ◆ Content knowledge influences comprehension.
- ◆ Content learning focuses on more than learning facts; it is information processing.

On-Ramp to Learning ▷ **Content Learning Goals**

- ◆ Entwine knowledge development with comprehension strategies.
- ◆ Focus on teaching reading through content.
- ◆ Develop a mental model to understand facts.
- ◆ Begin by tapping students' previous knowledge and adding to their knowledge "bank."

PART I

The Content-Rich Workshop

Teaching reading and writing through content is a shift in our practice and thinking. Shifting is difficult; it requires us to think in ways that we may not be able to visualize. Perhaps right now you are having trouble visualizing what the workshop would look like or how it would sound and what children might be doing. Give yourself time to think and process this model by reading and rereading parts of this book. To review how the workshop would look, refer to Figures 4.1 and 5.1 in Chapters 4 and 5. To think about how the workshop would sound and what children might be doing, refer to the protocols in Chapter 6. To develop your expertise in making your teaching transparent, refer to Chapters 4 and 7. Most of all, take time to browse the children's nonfiction section of your local library and take in what the informational texts offer. The publishers themselves are the best resource for engaging and exciting informational texts at a range of reading levels. A few series that offer outstanding materials are listed in Appendix A.

Overall, the goal is for children to develop domain knowledge in a variety of areas. They need to know a great deal about the world and our history in order to develop into mature readers and thinkers. Children deserve the opportunity to *know* everything they need to know to be competent in reading and writing. So does the content-based workshop give children the opportunity to learn the core reading and writing skills they need? Yes, they learn how to decode, how to read fluently, and how to comprehend. Yes, they learn how to spell, write grammatically correct pieces, and relate information and ideas to the world. Yes, they develop prior knowledge to understand text and prepare for new learning. Most of all, yes, they learn to become sophisticated readers who predict, question, visualize, clarify, and summarize while they read material that fills them with yearning to learn more. See Figure I.1, on page 13.

Content-based workshops develop this important knowledge work. It is imperative we leave behind the numerous weeks we spend focused only on strategies and turn to the specific content that should be taught at our grade level. *How* we do this is of the utmost importance. Fabulous units of study help children develop declarative knowledge and give them the opportunity to develop conscious and unconscious knowledge along the way. Let's begin.

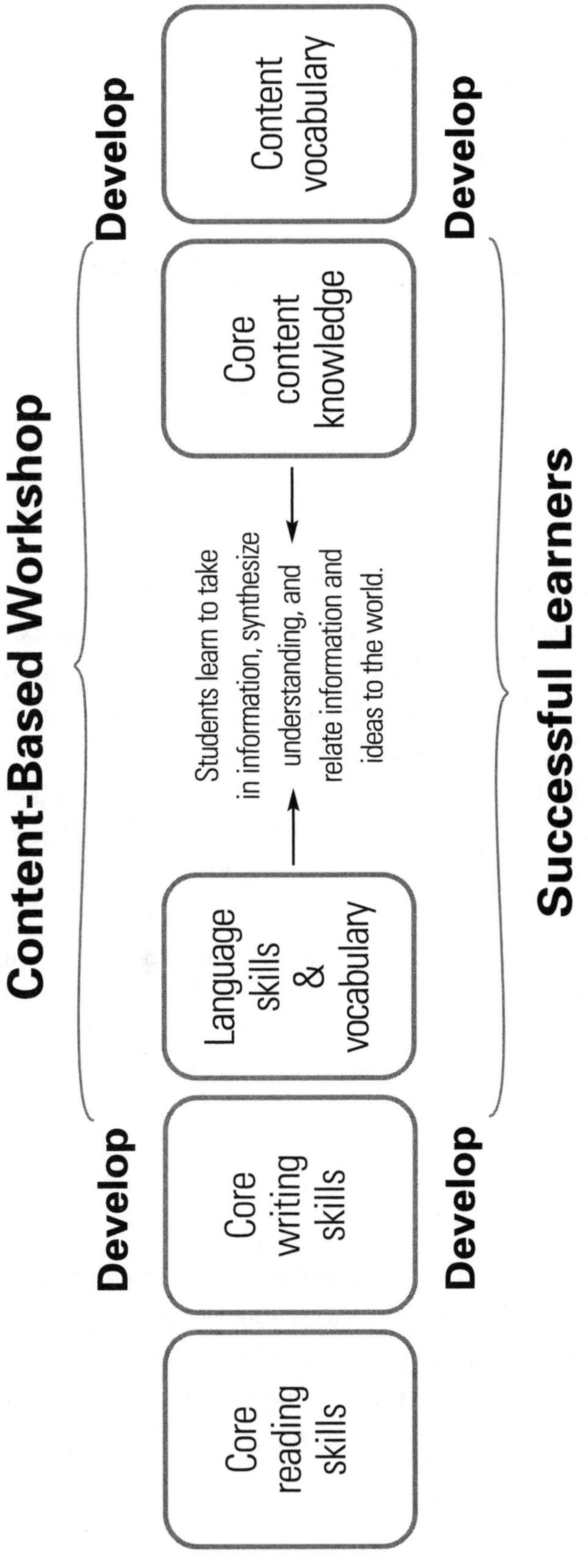

Content-Based Workshop

Develop

Core reading skills	Core writing skills	Language skills & vocabulary

Students learn to take in information, synthesize understanding, and relate information and ideas to the world.

Core content knowledge	Content vocabulary

Develop

Successful Learners

Develop   **Develop**

Figure I.1: The content-based workshop

CHAPTER 1

Activate Content Knowledge

Prereading Strategies That Engage the Brain

When you launch your first few units tying together content and comprehension, you are going to ensure that children know *how* to access texts. When they can access texts, they skim and scan chapters before reading, glean information from charts and diagrams, note bold words, and rehearse these new words in their minds. They gear up their brains. The first activities that connect children to content are prereading strategies. These strategies lay out a roadmap for children to independently grasp information, read it, and understand. This chapter suggests activities you can focus on *before* children read, before children grab the computer to research a topic, and before you send them off to "study" for a test.

Kids need to read, and they need to read a lot. By reading often and reading widely children develop the following essential qualities:

- Stamina

- Vocabulary

- Knowledge

- Power

Yes, power. Information is power and reading is the single most prevalent way for children to gain access. I don't remember the last time I saw reading occur during the time of day allotted for science and social studies in middle-grade classrooms. I am talking about *real* reading, where children enter the zone and get lost in the text and information (Atwell, 2007). Most often, I see children reading to fill out a work sheet or to answer the end-of-chapter questions.

This isn't real reading; this isn't powerful reading. This isn't the reading that will develop broad knowledge, and remember, as children develop broad knowledge, it is easier for them to comprehend a variety of texts (Trabasso & Bouchard, 2002; Tierney & Cunningham, 2002). The best way to improve reading ability, and the best way to improve content knowledge and vocabulary, is to read. Simply put, devoting time and attention to reading is the most important thing we can do for children (Allington, 2001).

Connecting technology-engaged youth and teens to content reading is, unfortunately, a complicated matter. We can begin to address the issue by moving what we normally do in postreading activities to prereading activities (or better yet, a focus on prereading strategies). Then instead of having children spend time discussing a text *after* reading it to see that they *didn't* comprehend it, we can prepare children to read and improve their ability to read the text. This way, great strategies that often go overlooked or *undone* become regular strategies that prepare and guide children through new avenues and text types.

Three effective strategies that work well as prereading activities are predicting, connecting, and organizing information (Moore, Readence, & Rickleman, 1989). These three strategies are shown to help all students comprehend texts better.

Prereading activities need to be targeted and effective. Just doing the activity isn't enough; the kids have to understand what they are doing and why they are doing it. I've often targeted a social studies lesson and carefully followed the prereading activities outlined in the teacher's manual. For a long time I didn't question *why* I needed to do the prereading activities; I just did them because I was supposed to—*after all*, they were listed in the teacher's manual. Eventually, the prereading activities took longer and longer, and at one point I spent more time with the prereading work than the actual reading. Before I knew it, my students were doing a lot of activities about reading, or activities, to prepare to read, and not ever really reading. I had to step back and take a long look at my instruction and remember that my goal was to develop better readers, not children who knew how to fill out graphic organizers without ever reading a word! The use of prereading tools is not an end in itself (I had *that* wrong for a long time) but rather the means to an end: children who comprehend what they *read*.

Kids in our classrooms first need to be engaged with content, and then they need reading strategies to help them navigate while reading texts varying in difficulty. The power of engagement is obvious as we observe students working with newer types of media, where they pick up new learning quickly. (By the time it takes me to figure out a new function on my computer, hours have passed, but my students figure it out in a snap). Our job, then, is to give them the academic floaters to be successful and remain engaged. It is a reinforcing process.

(See Figure 1.1.) When students engage with information and text and receive support, difficult content is easier to undertake; as a result, children develop understanding and experience success, which in turn leads to engagement.

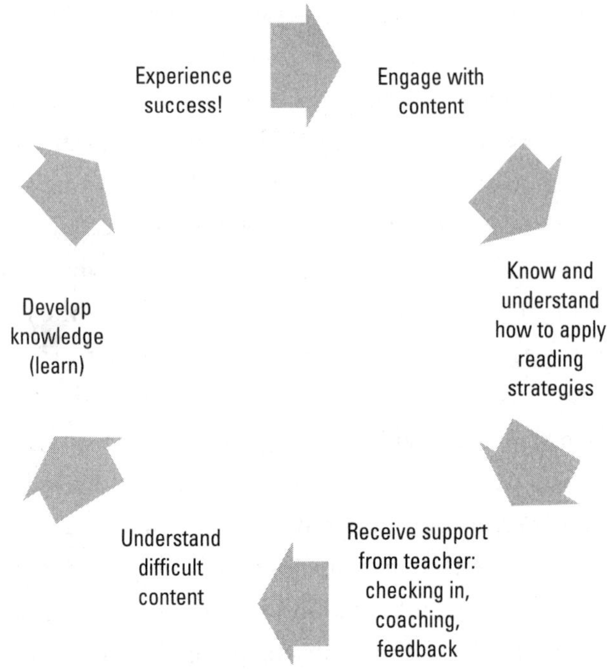

Prereading activities are designed to demystify content reading for students. Some children believe that they don't "get it" because they aren't capable. Often, they haven't had the opportunity to learn the "it" yet. Our self-efficacy would falter too, if we were expected to perform a task that we hadn't yet learned. So, to make content reading an enjoyable experience for all students, focus on directing children to the following points before reading text (Guthrie, 2003; Moore et al., 1989):

Figure 1.1: Reinforcing process

- Have a goal.
- Understand the text structure of a selection.
- Activate content knowledge.
- Develop a *tad* of content knowledge.

Have a Goal

Most students approach content reading like a novel: they start with word one and end on the assigned page or section. Let's see how well this works with two different texts: *Sea Critters* and *Rosa Parks*.

Figure 1.2: *Sea Critters*

"Water is magical! All creatures, large and small, must have it, from those living in the deepest seas to those who live in the highest trees. Nearly all of the Earth's water—97 percent—is ocean. It's an ocean filled with life! Sea critters abound, making every spoonful a kind of living soup."

Hmmm, if I were a kid, I might be thinking *Sea Critters* is about water and soup. (See Figure 1.2 on page 16.) So far, using only the text isn't helping me to understand what the book is going to be about. Now, based on the title, I know the book is about critters that live in the sea. I know from flipping through the pages that each page spread (both pages across) is about a different sea animal or type of sea animal.

So, after checking the first 50 words and looking at the structure of the book, a good goal would be to read the introduction; then read the first two classifications, "Animals with Holes" and "Stingers"; and then stop and check that I understand what I have read.

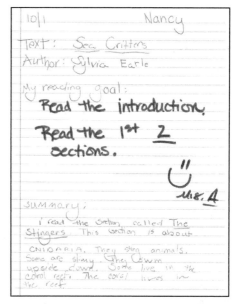

Figure 1.3: Student goal for *Sea Critters*

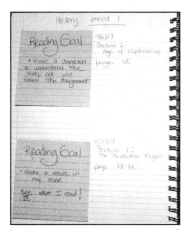

Figure 1.4: Student notebook with reading goals

Figure 1.3 shows a student's goals for *Sea Critters*. I can write the goal out, too, and put it in my notebook. (I have students write their goal on a sticky sheet, like a name tag or large address label, and place it in their notebooks. I also add reading goals to students' notebooks this way. See Figure 1.4 for an example.

Students reading at a higher reading level may undertake a book such as *Rosa Parks* from the African American Biographies series.

The first paragraph of *Rosa Parks* states:

"Rosa Parks was an ordinary African-American woman in 1955, when she changed history. She was 42 years old and working in a department store in Montgomery, Alabama. At the time, the front section of buses was reserved for white riders only. African-American riders had to ride in the back section. But one day after work, Rosa decided not to give up her seat. She was tired of being treated badly because of the color of her skin. So she refused to stand up, and she was arrested. . . . By refusing to give up her seat, Rosa Parks began a chain of events that led to better treatment for all African-Americans."

While this text is clearly written and sets up the reader to anticipate the content of the book, for many readers it would not be effective to just begin reading on the first page and go straight through to the end. The book includes several features to aid comprehension, including a large index and several text boxes. From the first paragraph, I would expect the book to tell about the chain of events that changed the lives of African Americans, and the way in which Rosa Parks created this momentum, so I am not worried about the clarity of the text. After flipping through the pages in the book, I realize that a challenge for readers of this text would be its length. The book is 64 pages long and each page is dense with text. If I were thinking like a student, I might consider a good reading goal

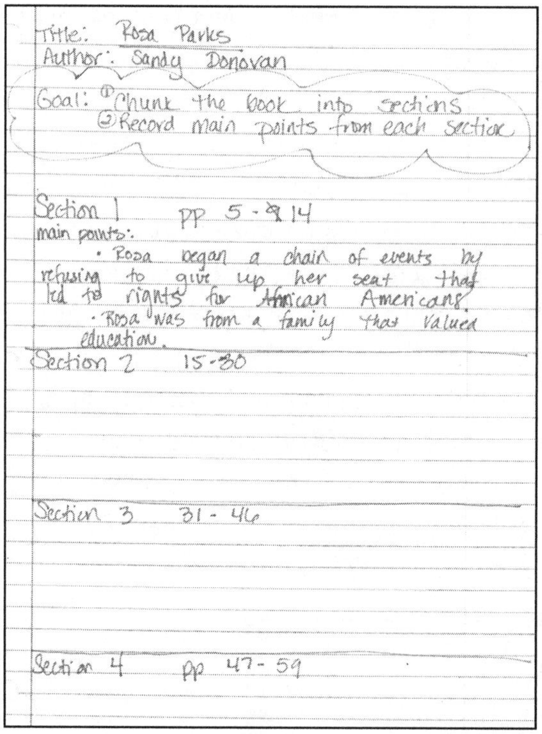

Figure 1.5: Student goal for *Rosa Parks*

to be to chunk the book into sections and then record the main points from each section in my notebook. I could set up my notebook page by dividing it into sections where I list the information from each book section. I would write this goal in my notebook. (See Figure 1.5.)

Teach children to have a goal figured out before they begin reading. They might consider one or more of these:

- What they expect to learn from the text
- How the organization of the text helps them comprehend what the text is saying
- What strategy they will use to remember information while reading
- How much they will read in one sitting

The Content-Rich Reading & Writing Workshop

Having a goal gives students these advantages:

- Focus: "I am going to need to . . . "

- An end point to aim for: "I can read, just a bit more, even though I feel like giving up, because I only have to get to . . . "

- Purpose: "I am reading this so I can . . . "

- Connection: "How does this idea or information connect to what I already know about . . . ?"

Understand Text Structure

Content sources and nonfiction pieces are designed in unique ways, depending on subject matter and type of text. A nonfiction library book is different from a textbook, which is different from a nonfiction narrative. Teach students to survey a text before reading to understand its structure. By understanding the structure, students are less confused when reading, as they can refer back to it, think through discrepancies in their reading, and observe how the information is laid out (Moore et al., 1989; Pappas, 2006). In this manner, they can be in control of their reading. If a student can predict a pattern by flipping pages and scanning text layout, then she can focus on what the text is saying and not get overly distracted by the text boxes, bold print, and other add-ons. This focus can help a child move beyond word-by-word processing and focus on meaning. Children who process word by word are so focused on decoding and maintaining some fluency that they cannot retain meaning in short-term memory (Farstrup, 2002; Schwanenflugel et al., 2006; Stahl & Heubach, 2006). A text might be structured as one of the following types:

- List

- Problem-solution

- Cause and effect

- Description

- Persuasive

Paying systematic attention to the underlying text organization helps students relate ideas in ways that make them more understandable and more memorable (Duke & Pearson 2002). With multiple experiences this develops a general understanding of how texts tend to be structured within specific content areas. Children come to realize that social studies texts often have a specific type of structure, as do many scientific texts.

List

This text selection from the teacher's edition of *Scholastic News* is part of an article titled "Gyms for Kids" (2007). The text on either side of the nutrition chart is written as a list. (See Figure 1.6.)

Figure 1.6: Example of list structure

Some texts are written entirely as a list. For example, the leveled nonfiction text by Benchmark Education *Working With Electricity and Magnetism* (Furgang, 2004) is written in a list structure. The information on each page is listed separately from information on previous or following pages. Each section has a heading stating what it is about. The text in each section doesn't refer to any information in a previous section, so a student could read each section independently. In this book the section headings are: static electricity, current electricity, magnetism, and electromagnetism. The title and structure of the book hold the information together.

List books are often less sophisticated than other content books, texts, and articles. The list structure provides a large amount of information and facts in a small amount of text. Most reference texts are designed in a list structure. List structures often provide the following features:

- Information and facts are organized in a consistent manner, for example, alphabetical or subhead order.

- Some information stands alone. Sections are not necessarily related; each section may be independent of information in previous sections.

- Indexes and glossaries enable students to look up information and then refer to details in text.

Problem-Solution

The text "Indy-pendent Fuel: Retooled race cars leave harmful fumes in the dust" (Meanley, 2007), an article from *Scope* classroom magazine, is organized in a problem-solution structure. (See Figure 1.7.)

Figure 1.7: "Indy-pendent Fuel: Retooled race cars leave harmful fumes in the dust" from *Scope*

In this article, the information near the beginning describes the problem: Human activity is the cause of global warming. Governments are urged to order the slashing of emissions. The body of the text provides information about the solution. The article makes the point that ethanol is a solution to inefficient fuel consumption and won't ruin the environment in the same ways as petroleum products.

Texts structured as problem-solution begin by setting up a situation and discussing the problem. Then the text presents the solution, stating facts and referencing theory, experience, and research to substantiate it. Some texts are written in a problem-solution pattern where one problem is presented and then solved. More sophisticated texts present a succession of solutions to a complex problem, or interrelated problems presented in succession, for example:

Problem 1 ——————→ Solution and/or subsequent issue
Problem 2 ——————→ Solution

These texts include an overall conclusion that wraps up the solution to the problems presented. Often the conclusion may reference the need for further study or research.

Cause and Effect

A section of the book *Building Bridges* by Kathy Furgang (2004) is organized in a cause-and-effect layout.

On page 18 the first paragraph states: "The Tacoma Narrows Bridge across Puget Sound in Washington was designed to be very flexible. It turned out to be too flexible." Then the text provides the effect: "The bridge twisted in the wind for hours. The violent twisting strained the bridge enough to make it collapse." The remaining texts, photos, and fact boxes provide additional information about other causes and effects related to bridges.

Texts structured as cause and effect identify sources of a problem or issue in an orderly way. More sophisticated texts may list multiple causes and effects to describe a situation. For example, when studying the Civil War in fifth grade, students begin to expand their learning about the causes of the war. I always smile when a student comes running up to me in the hallway, wide-eyed, and tells me that the war was about more than slavery. As children mature, they are ready for texts that give more than one angle to explain an issue.

Texts with multiple viewpoints are more challenging for inexperienced readers than texts that describe a single cause and effect. It is common for textbooks to outline a historical event by listing multiple reasons for it. As students face informational texts with depth, they will have the opportunity to read historical documents and a variety of sources to understand an issue. Often, this supplemental information is included in textbooks and trade books, providing multiple perspectives on the same issue. Therefore, readers need to understand that the causes of an event may not be straightforward, and identifying those in the text will help them understand their reading.

Description

The online article "Investigate the Giant Squid: Mysterious Cephalopod of the Sea" (Scholastic, 2007) includes a lot of information arranged by subheading. Overall this web-based text describes information related to coelenterates, or soft-bodied sea creatures, including body structure, body forms, reproduction, and types of coelenterates. (See Figure 1.8.)

Figure 1.8: "Investigate the Giant Squid: Mysterious Cephalopod of the Sea"

Descriptive texts are common structures found in a variety of sources, including magazines, trade books, library books, leveled texts, and textbooks. Magazine articles, newspaper articles, and classroom periodicals (such as *Time for Kids* or *Scholastic News*) are often written as descriptive texts. While the author's intent and opinion may be apparent in the writing, descriptive texts don't aim at changing the reader's opinion or viewpoint on the subject.

Children need to identify the structure of ideas and the relationship of one idea to another. In most descriptive texts a hierarchical order of ideas exists. In other words, not every sentence is as important as the others. When I was in college, before I learned how to determine what was most important, I used to highlight virtually the entire text. I see this so often with children as they learn to use highlighters to underline parts of text. Often, the entire piece they read turns yellow, green, or blue. Children have to learn to quickly distinguish more important ideas from less important ideas (Farstrup, 2002; Vacca, 2002). This is important when they learn to highlight and take notes.

When I first began teaching text structure, I fell into the "main idea" trap. I thought the point was for students to identify the main idea and nothing else. This point was especially important when *identifying the main idea in text* became part of English language arts standards in California (where I teach and work). I have seen a plethora of teaching materials designed to show us the golden rule of teaching the main idea. The truth of the matter is that there is no secret formula for identifying the main idea in text, and children actually need to do more than just find it. They need to determine *importance* in text, a research-based strategy that helps them comprehend and, of course, identify main ideas.

To determine importance in text, children's reading skills must go beyond finding the main idea (which, by the way, doesn't *always* appear at the beginning of a paragraph). They need to be able to hold ideas they read in their minds long enough to figure out what information in a paragraph or series of paragraphs is the most important to remember and know. Children need to know how to sort and select while reading.

Persuasive

An advertisement appearing in the magazine *Defenders: The Conservation Magazine of Defenders of Wildlife* is a persuasive text. It tries to convince the reader to give money in order to protect polar bears.

The text begins:

"Global warming is causing the loss of critical sea ice needed by polar bears, and aggressive hunting by humans and environmental contamination are pushing polar bears further to the brink of extinction."

The final paragraph reads:

"Please help Defenders of Wildlife ensure future generations of bears will have more habitat range than a few zoos scattered around the world."

Then the text goes on to urge the reader to send a petition to Congress and a donation to the organization.

Let the fun begin! Exploring persuasive texts and the reasoning behind the words is interesting and intriguing to students. Your standards may state that students need to identify fallacious (false) reasoning or supportive reasoning in text. For example, the California ELA standards for sixth grade state the following: "Note instances of unsupported inferences, fallacious reasoning, persuasion, and propaganda in text" (California State Board of Education, 2007).

Once children understand what fallacious reasoning is, they usually run with it, identifying false thinking or persuasive thinking with a weak connection wherever they can find it. In one sixth-grade class I worked with, the children created fallacious reasoning notebooks. They scoured magazines for examples and wrote about how the ads enticed readers to buy a product because it promised to do something wonderful. (You know the thinking: drink diet soda and be thin!) Of course, there are many types of persuasive texts, but beginning by teaching the persuasion in advertisements is engaging for children and helps them quickly see the persuasive argument. Children do need to identify persuasive thinking in a variety of formats. It helps them see how the buildup of information generally leads to a conclusion designed to get the reader to change his or her mind about an issue.

Activate Content Knowledge

Before children begin reading each day in the workshop, you need to wake up their brains, to stimulate their thinking and get their thinking muscles ready to go (Sousa, 2006). Do this by telling children the following:

- What they are going to read

- Why they are reading it

- How the information they already know about the subject relates to the new information

These three simple steps can make all the difference in the world. Consider the article "How the Brain Learns Best" by Bruce Perry (2007). (See Figure 1.9 on page 26.) Before reading the text, we need to prepare ourselves to read by considering the following:

- *The What*
  We are going to read about how our brains learn and how attention affects learning. The text structure is descriptive. Perry tells how learning requires attention and then gives recommendations for instruction.

- *The Why*
  This is important because we can adapt Perry's recommendations to our teaching. He provides a few tips on how to maximize student attention so that children can learn the most from our lessons.

- *The How*
  We already know quite a bit about how the children in our classrooms learn. You may notice that some children have different strengths than others, or you may notice that after a few minutes of direct instruction the attention of your class wanes. What are other things you know about how the children learn in your classroom?

The *what, why, how* frame jogged your thinking before you read (at least, I hope it did!). When our brains are primed and awake, it is easier to concentrate on the reading and retain information. In short, the *what, why, how* frame is a protocol, or expected framework (refer to Chapter 6 for a discussion of protocols), that stimulates the part of your brain that *knows* about learning and brain development.

Often students really do know—sometimes they haven't had time to get their thinking muscles working; other times they might be too shy to tell the class. Change the situation by reminding the children yourself. It helps them remember before you are halfway through teaching the lesson that they do know something about the subject, and when you share a quick snippet of info, you are keeping the prereading conversation focused and timely—not letting the conversation be dominated by the one child in class who loves to talk a lot or skipping the conversation because the children are too shy to talk.

The Essence of Connection

Our brains catalog important information in webs of interconnected ideas and we recall information in the same manner. Let's experiment with this for a moment. Take a blank piece of paper at least 8½ by 11 inches and draw a circle in the middle. Inside the circle write the title of a geographical feature that you live near or love. I love the ocean, so my

How the Brain Learns Best   Dr. Bruce Perry

Easy ways to gain optimal learning in the classroom by activating different parts of the brain

By Bruce D. Perry, M.D., Ph.D.

Over the last 40 years we have learned more about the human brain than in the previous 400 years. Educators and neuroscientists have been trying to put this knowledge to work by transforming the information of basic and clinical neurosciences into practical insights for the classroom. In a series of special features, we will be looking at how the brain works and what this can tell us about your teaching.

First, however, it is important to remember that all learning is brain-based. Through the process of education, we are trying literally to change the brain — not the pancreas, spleen, or lungs. Indeed, education is practical neuroscience. That does not mean that every teacher needs to become a neuroscientist or memorize 100 neurotransmitters and 50 brain areas responsible for cognition. But it does mean that teachers can become more effective with some knowledge of how the brain senses, processes, stores, and retrieves information.

Neural System Fatigue

Learning requires attention. And attention is mediated by specific parts of the brain. Yet, neural systems fatigue quickly, actually within minutes. With three to five minutes of sustained activity, neurons become "less responsive"; they need a rest (not unlike our muscles when you lift weights). They can recover within minutes too, but when they are stimulated in a sustained way, they just are not as efficient. Think about the piano and the organ; if you put your finger on the organ key and hold it down it will keep making noise, but the piano key makes one short note, and keeping your finger there produces no more sound. Neurons are like pianos, not organs. They respond to patterned and repetitive, rather than to sustained, continuous stimulation. Why is this important for a teacher?

When a child listens as you say, "George Washington was 6'4" tall," she uses one neural system (call it A). When she is told about a concept related to that fact ("The average height of men during the Revolutionary War was only 5'4"," a slightly different, but functionally interconnected neural set (B) is used. When she listens to a vignette: "Washington, at the darkest moment in the Revolution, when his soldiers were deep in the despair of defeat, starving and freezing at Valley Forge, slowly rose to his full height and, using his dominant personality (in part conveyed by his physical dominance) and was able to motivate his discouraged soldiers to re-enlist and continue fighting," yet other related neural systems are active (C and D). These interrelated neural systems are all important in learning; indeed, our students will learn more completely if they make "changes" (create memory) in all of these neural systems (A, B, C, and D). Facts are empty without being linked to context and concepts.

When a child is in a familiar and safe situation, as in most of our classrooms, his or her brain will seek novelty. So, if this child hears only factual information, she will fatigue within minutes. Only four to eight minutes of pure factual lecture can be tolerated before the brain seeks other stimuli, either internal (e.g., daydreaming) or external (Who is that walking down the hall?). If the teacher is not providing that novelty, the brain will go elsewhere. Continuous presentation of facts or concepts in isolation or in a nonstop series of anecdotes will all have the same fatiguing effect — and the child will not learn as much, nor will she come to anticipate and enjoy learning.

The best presentation, the most engaging and effective teaching, has all three elements. And it is very important how the teacher puts these elements together.

The Bob-and-Weave Lecture

The most effective presentation must move back and forth through these interrelated neural systems, weaving them together. These areas are interconnected under usual circumstances, like a complete "workout" in the gym where we rotate from one station to another. Similarly, in teaching, it is most effective to work one neural area and then move on to another. Engage your students with a story to provide the context. Make sure this vignette can touch the emotional parts of their brains. This will activate and prepare the cognitive parts of the brain for storing information. Information is easiest to digest when there is emotional "seasoning" — humor, empathy, sadness, and fear all make "dry" facts easier to swallow. Give a fact or two; link these facts into related concepts. Move back to the narrative to help them make the connection between this concept and the story. Go back to another fact. Reinforce the concepts. Reconnect with the original story. In and out, bob and weave, among facts, concept, and narrative.

Human beings are storytelling primates. We are curious, and we love to learn. The challenge for each teacher is to find ways to engage the child and take advantage of the novelty-seeking property of the human brain to facilitate learning.

*This article orginally appeared in *Instructor* magazine.

Dr. Bruce D. Perry, M.D., Ph.D., is an internationally recognized authority on brain development and children in crisis. Dr. Perry leads the ChildTrauma Academy, a pioneering center providing service, research and training in the area of child maltreatment (www.ChildTrauma.org). In addition he is the Medical Director for Provincial Programs in Children's Mental Health for Alberta, Canada. Dr. Perry served as consultant on many high-profile incidents involving traumatized children, including the Columbine High School shootings in Littleton, Colorado; the Oklahoma City Bombing; and the Branch Davidian siege. His clinical research and practice focuses on traumatized children-examining the long-term effects of trauma in children, adolescents and adults. Dr. Perry's work has been instrumental in describing how traumatic events in childhood change the biology of the brain. The author of more than 200 journal articles, book chapters, and scientific proceedings and is the recipient of a variety of professional awards.

Figure 1.9: "How the Brain Learns Best"

example says *ocean*. (See Figure 1.10.) If you live in or near the mountains, a prairie, a river, flatlands, the ocean, grasslands, foothills, whatever the case, write the word in the circle. Now, as quickly as you can, list everything that comes to mind about the feature you chose. Put each thing you think of in a smaller circle connected to the central circle. If these ideas generate other associations, branch even smaller circles off from them. As your thinking slows down, don't stop—keep pushing for other associations you make. Work at this for about three to four minutes.

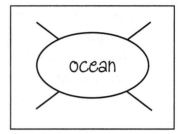

Figure 1.10: Web with center circle filled in

How many different things did you associate with the geographical feature that you wrote down initially? It is interesting how our brains connect ideas and information and how retrieval of information can often be connected to things that we wouldn't associate consciously (Zull, 2002). For example, in my web (see Figure 1.11), I associated *crystal* with *ocean* because my daughter once found a fully formed crystal about 6 inches long on the beach. Now that isn't your everyday association with oceans, but if I were reading about land formation underwater, remembering that day we found the crystal would "wake up my brain" a bit and prepare me to read more.

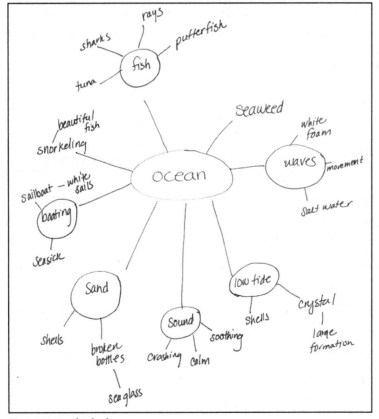

Figure 1.11: Completed web

If your students don't have any background knowledge to tap that will help them as they read, then spend a few (a very few) minutes giving some background knowledge. You can create a class web or begin a K-W-L chart with the whole group so that the class benefits from the information that other children in the class know and can share (Neufeld, 2005). Notice I said "a very few" minutes building background knowledge prior to reading. Keep your focus on the reading and what children will learn *while* reading. In prereading activities, you just want to wake up their brains and get them ready. If they don't know, then they will learn as they read and write about their reading. Remember that you don't want to spend so much time on a prereading activity that you commit these errors:

- Waste minutes children could spend reading
- Bore the class with too much information
- Make the prereading activity more important than reading

Develop Knowledge

When kids know a lot about various subjects, historical facts, issues, places, and people, they are better readers. The same point applies to all of us adult readers as well. The more we know, the more we can connect to text, the easier it is to understand what we read, the more we retain what we read, and so the process goes. The more information we know, the better readers we become (Anderson & Pearson, 1984; Gaskins, 1996). So, let's keep going—it is time to build "during reading" strategies into our instruction.

On-Ramp to Learning ▸ **Focus on the Speed of Learning**

- ◆ Instruction should target what students need to know and move at an engaging pace.
- ◆ Assess first so you don't teach what they already know.
- ◆ Use assessment results to teach within students' reach—not moving so fast that learning is out of their grasp, but moving at a pace that makes them stretch.
- ◆ Engage students by waking up their brains, showing them, and reinforcing your lessons.

CHAPTER 2

Crack Open Informational Text

Learning Content While Learning to Read

Remember that some days during your content-based workshop you will focus on content and the learning strategies to help children remember, and other days you will be focused on teaching reading through content. The conventional wisdom that children learn to read by third grade and then spend their lives reading to learn, isn't true. Children continue to learn to read as they grow, face new materials, see new content, and experience new literacies. When working with children who can read, and children still learning to read, our focus includes two things (Gaskins, 1996):

■ Teaching children to read all types of materials, with attention to accuracy, fluency, and motivation

■ Ensuring that children learn information while reading

Teaching Children to Read Better: Accuracy, Fluency, and Motivation

Entire books are written on this subject, and I am not going to attempt to address all the information that you may need to know to teach children to improve their accuracy, fluency, and reading motivation, as there are excellent resources for you to explore in this area. I am going to suggest a few techniques and teaching strategies that work—big structures to consider putting in place in your classroom that can buoy student motivation, desire to read, and understanding.

Kids who excel at school read approximately 30 minutes per day. This means they are seeing many words per day, connecting to new ideas and materials each time they read.

These kids are learning. On the other hand, struggling readers *actually* read about five minutes per day (Allington, 2001). They spend most of their time *preparing* to read. Instead, they need to just read. The classroom setting should buoy their efforts and reinforce intrinsic motivation, or their desire to read.

Accuracy and Text Levels

Most standards documents list a goal for student reading ability in terms of accuracy and fluency. For example, the California language arts fifth-grade reading standard for word recognition states that students should be able to "read aloud narrative and expository text fluently and accurately and with appropriate pacing, intonation, and expression" (California State Board of Education, 2007). Another example of a standard focused on accuracy and fluency is the sixth-grade reading goal from South Carolina: "The student will draw upon a variety of strategies to comprehend, interpret, analyze, what he or she reads" (South Carolina Department of Education, 2007).

The expectations for these standards seem straightforward enough. We might think, "Okay, my students need to read the textbook independently by the end of the year, so let's get started and move on through!" Teaching would be so much simpler if textbooks and other materials were designed on a developmental gradient, but, of course, they aren't. Even if textbooks were written at a reading level specific to the grade level they address, they can't match the needs of all readers. That is our job. This issue creates two things to be aware of: first, students need to practice reading in texts that provide an appropriate challenge; second, textbooks have a variety of reading selections that represent a range of text levels.

In a study that looked at various reading recommendations for third-grade readers and their text levels, Hiebert (2002) found that there is a wide variance in the text levels of various reading recommendations made in standards documents. The study compared texts in three ways, by levels in the Lexile Framework for reading, by levels established by the Fountas and Pinnell Benchmark Assessment System, and by grade level as identified by the publisher. The findings showed a wide variety of text levels in recommended readings for third graders, ranging from Lexile levels 430 to 1010, also defined in reading levels as grades 2.3 to 9.3. Overall, the text levels of recommended reading were challenging. This is important to note as we should not assign independent reading to children from texts and textbooks solely by the grade level identified on the spine or heading of the text.

Fluency

Fluent readers can read orally with speed, accuracy, and proper expression (Samuels, 2002). Children who are fluent are able to pay attention to the meaning of text without having to overly focus on identifying words. Fluency has gained importance in teaching reading in the last few years, and with good reason. It should not be ignored in the content-based workshop, but it is important to understand the role of fluency on comprehension.

It isn't enough to simply focus on increasing the ability of children in upper grades to decode text rapidly; they need to be fluent in comprehension processing as well. Skilled readers make inferences automatically and instantaneously while reading, which helps them construct a coherent representation of text (Hasbrouck & Tindal, 2006; Samuels, 2002). Therefore, for older students, fluency includes rapid decoding of text and rapid generation of inferences, comparisons to reader knowledge, and processing of information. Focusing only on timing students' fluency by having them read passages is not enough to help older students improve their reading rates; they need opportunities to practice with materials that are motivating to read and have meaning for them. Repeated reading of content materials helps students improve their reading rates and can help them improve their overall reading ability (Rasinski et al., 2005). Helpful techniques for improving upper-grade students' fluency include the following:

AR ➡ Wide reading of independent-level texts

Lit Circles ➡ Guided reading of instructional-level texts

? ➡ Repeated readings of texts already previewed

Drama strand ➡ "Performed" repeated readings such as Readers Theater or shared reading

? ➡ Assisted reading, in which students read aloud while simultaneously listening to a fluent reader read the same text (Rasinski et al., 2005; Rasinski, 2003)

Motivation

As I said before, the best way for children to improve their reading ability is to read. But no one is motivated to read texts that are too hard, and reading difficult texts doesn't make us smarter or better readers—instead, it makes us frustrated readers.

Let's consider for a minute how our brains work when reading something we may be unfamiliar with. Now, the text we are going to read is definitely from a subject I am unfamiliar with, and I don't have the conceptual understanding to comprehend this text on a first read. In fact, when I reread it several times, I just begin to grasp what the text *might* be saying.

> *The same mechanism is present at the epidermal-connective tissue junction.*
> *The epithelial cells are affixed to the connective tissue by means of the electron*
> *microscope basal lamina, yet they can detach and migrate toward the surface."*
> *(Grant, Stern, & Everett, 1979)*

I found this short text difficult to read, and I consider myself a good reader without problems in accuracy and fluency when I read most texts. But when I read this text from a dentistry textbook, my reading rate fell and I paused often. I had to stop and silently sound out *epithelial*. Though I know what the words *mechanism* and *junction* mean, figuring out how they relate in this text was difficult, and I had to reread the first sentence several times. After reading this paragraph three times, I am still not sure how to pronounce some of the words correctly, much less what they mean. Honestly, after reading this, and really trying to comprehend the meaning, I was distracted and began to think of everything else I could do besides read that paragraph. My mind wandered.

So while it is important that students have the opportunity to read daily, they need to be matched to texts that they can read (decode) and understand (comprehend). Students will be motivated to read content if it makes sense to them and if they feel successful (Duke & Pearson, 2002; Fountas & Pinnell, 2006). In content reading, however, we don't always have the choice, or opportunity, to match students' reading ability to texts, so awareness is important. By knowing and understanding the reading abilities of our students, we can be sensitive to their instructional needs when assigning texts to be read independently (Hiebert, 2002).

Supporting Readers With Texts

It is not only inappropriate but also unproductive to assign reading that is beyond your students' instructional reading levels. Now, I am not saying that you shouldn't ever give students assignments based on text above their reading level—the truth is it happens from time to time—but that is what scaffolds are for. When children do need to read above-grade-level texts and beyond their instructional level, assign them appropriately and give support. Instead of focusing on teaching reading from these texts, focus on teaching a learning strategy and having children gather information (Grasser, McNamara, & Louwerse, 2003). (This is addressed in Chapter 6, beginning on page 92.) When we teach reading using nonfiction texts, we are focused on reading and reading strategies. This is when children need to be in a text that matches their instructional needs.

Instructional level, as measured by running records, an assessment involving listening to children read aloud and noting the mistakes they make, is generally defined as reading 92 to 97 percent of the words correctly. A text is considered at a student's independent level when he or she reads 97 to 100 percent of words correctly. Anything below 92 percent is considered to be at a student's frustration level. In other words, if a student makes 8 to 9 mistakes or more in a 100-word passage, the text is too hard for him to read independently, or in guided reading (Fountas & Pinnell, 1996; Vellutino, 2003).

So, you might be wondering, how do students ever get to grade level? Don't they have to be exposed to "grade level" texts to meet standards? The answer is yes and no. Children need to be exposed to and learn the content expected for each grade level as outlined in state curriculum documents, but struggling readers won't learn to read better by being *required* to read "grade level" texts. In fact, the experience may be so negative that children will not want to read at all. And the less they read, the less proficient they become at reading, while their peers who can and do read just become better and better.

Sustenance for All Readers

Supporting readers requires us to design foundations to accelerate their learning and keep them on track whether they are struggling readers or children reading on grade level (Allington, 2001; Vellutino, 2003). All readers need the sustenance of reading instruction, no matter what grade level they are in. Oh, I know that may feel uncomfortable if you have been teaching in a grade level for a while where you didn't see yourself as a reading teacher. Don't despair! There are great strategies you can use in your classroom that will foster students' reading abilities without requiring you to take a course in teaching reading.

Develop student reading abilities in these three ways:

- Independent sustained reading

- Textbook reading with reading "tools"

- Leveled nonfiction/content book reading

Independent Sustained Reading (ISR)

Independent Sustained Reading is a time of day when children read *with a purpose* a text at their independent level, or a previously previewed text at their instructional level, and respond to the text in some way. Children may know that they are reading to practice a strategy taught during a mini-lesson (summarizing after each chapter or section, for example), and then after reading they will write in their reading response notebooks to practice the strategy. ISR is different from Silent Sustained Reading (SSR) because children are reading with a purpose; that is, they have a goal when they dive into the text (Akhavan, 2007). They are reading a text connected to a unit of study over several days; they don't jump around each day and grab a text because they have to have something to read. And they respond; they may talk through their ideas in a think/pair/share cooperative learning group prior to writing their responses (Neufeld, 2005; Vacca, 2002)

Plan for ISR in your reading workshop several times a week. If you teach middle school and see your students in short periods, plan short ISR sessions at the beginning of the period. I know, it may seem impossible to *waste* the short amount of time you have your students with independent reading, but remember, the best way for students to learn to read the content books your class demands, and the best way for them to improve their reading abilities, is to *read*.

In all classrooms, but especially in upper-grade classrooms, ISR is imperative. Where else but in class will students learn to read the texts, enjoy reading, and value reading as an activity that can enhance their lives and be a source of information? What we value and love as teachers, our students will value and love. We model for them in more ways than we can imagine, so provide time for reading. Abundant reading leads to growth in vocabulary and fluency over time (Samuels, 2002).

ISR isn't an idle time in your classroom during which nothing is going on. Students are selecting texts, thinking about their reading, and recording information that is important to know (Neufeld, 2005). They are *learning*. Remember that brain research tells us that learning is pleasurable—and a natural function that our brains seek. So, if children learn while reading, reading becomes pleasurable, not a pain. During ISR you are busy too. ISR isn't a drop-everything-and-read (DEAR) time, and you are not reading. As you meet with individuals and groups, you are taking notes about what they are reading, how they are progressing, and what strategies you see them using to help themselves learn. You may also be taking a running record or checking a text level to see that a child has correctly self-selected a text for ISR.

Materials that Support ISR

Children need access to a variety of texts. You can bring in books from the library, have content magazines available, or collect books from a variety of sources. There are fabulous leveled texts on a variety of subjects now available from many publishers. Perhaps you can ask your administrator to buy books your students can use for ISR and for research.

Children also need notebooks. The notebooks are reading logs where student can document what they read, how long they read, and how they responded. They may be jotting notes down on interesting tidbits of information they come across, things they want to remember, or words they don't know. Figure 2.1 on page 35 shows two pages from a student's notebook. On these pages the student recorded what she read, including the page numbers. She apparently read the same book out of class because the next day she began reading farther into the book during ISR. On the other page, she wrote down three words she had trouble with. By using this vocabulary sheet she evaluated her understanding of the word and wrote the page and the sentence the word came from. It appears that for the word *geologist*, she discussed the meaning with a friend or her teacher, as she wrote the definition in her own words to help her remember its meaning.

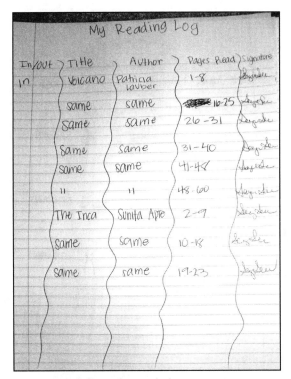

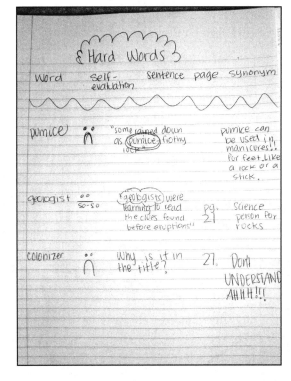

Figure 2.1: Sample from student's notebook

Reading notebooks can include reading logs, vocabulary organizers, and graphic organizers to help children focus on effective reading strategies.

Reading Notebook Contents

■ Reading logs: Figure 2.2 provides an example of a reading log page. (See Appendix B, page 132, for a reproducible.) Have students record the book, author, and pages read each day in class.

■ Vocabulary organizers: There are several ways to help children learn academic and content domain vocabulary.

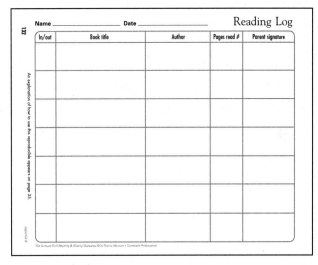

Figure 2.2: Reading log

Accelerated Vocabulary Instruction: Strategies for Closing the Achievement Gap for All Students (Akhavan, 2007) provides a variety of techniques and graphic organizers to ensure vocabulary growth. Figure 2.3 shows an example of a vocabulary log you can include in reading notebooks. Children can use the log to record unfamiliar words they encounter while reading. (See Appendix C, page 133, for a reproducible.)

Name _____		Date _____	Vocabulary Log—Words to Learn
Book Title _____			
Word	Self-evaluation * I know it * I don't know it	Sentence and page #	Synonym for the word

Figure 2.3: Vocabulary log

- Graphic organizers: There are multiple graphic organizers in Chapter 3 that can be used in student notebooks. Some of the strategies help students with reading comprehension and others help them learn facts.

Textbook Reading With Reading "Tools"

Josh, a young teacher, was a go-getter. His aim was clear: to increase the amount of science knowledge his fifth-grade students had. After all, the year before they didn't score well on the state standardized test, and there was so little time to teach science that the subject was often forgotten. But this year was different; Josh had a mission. Unfortunately, Josh had few resources available to him to teach science beyond the textbook, but he wasn't worried; he just jumped in with each unit and plowed his way through the curriculum as outlined in the teacher's manual.

When I had the opportunity to watch Josh teach his science lessons, it was March. His students were a bit distracted while he lectured from the textbook. In fact there were several things going on in class:

- The children who could read the book were reading ahead of Josh and not listening. Then when he was done teaching, they raised their hands for clarification on the points he had made and asked for help to understand the point of one section in the textbook.

- The children who couldn't read the book or follow Josh's lecture had "turned off and tuned out." These kids were trying to look as though they were listening, but when it came time to complete the assignment, two of them asked to go to the bathroom, and one student sat for about 10 minutes before attempting the work.

■ The children that were engaged were "on." These 10 or so students were raising their hands consistently, asking questions for clarification, and focusing on what Josh was saying while looking at the illustrations in the textbook. One student was writing down some of the terms Josh used. After the lesson, during the assignment, I sat with two or three of the students to help them complete their work. While they had listened attentively, the children asked me to repeat some of the information Josh had shared, as they were having trouble remembering the important points. They didn't know how to go back and read the information in the text; they were skimming, but getting distracted by unimportant points.

Josh's experience could have been my own when I was teaching. When I worked with the textbook, some children seemed to get it but then showed a lack of understanding, and others seemed to be very disconnected. It was obvious that they need to be taught how to read and use the textbook. Reading textbooks requires different skills than reading novels, library books, or magazines. Textbooks jam lots and lots of information in just a few pages, load up the text with many graphics, and sometimes seem to weight all information equally. Learning to navigate textbook reading is a must for children (Hansen & Pearson, 1983; Klinger & Vaughn, 2004).

Here are some things students can do:

■ Survey the text structures and text features

■ Identify key ideas

■ Take notes on key information items

■ Return to the text efficiently to reread, regroup, and remind themselves of key ideas

Textbook Tamer

The Textbook Tamer is a process students can follow when they're reading the textbook independently, rereading to clarify points from a lesson, or familiarizing themselves with information in the unit. Children need to be able to gather information from the textbook and make sense of that information. By showing them how to "tame" the textbook, you give children a frame of reference for textbook reading and help them by giving them strategies to glean important points from text.

The Textbook Tamer graphic organizer walks students through the steps of the text survey process. (See Figure 2.4 on page 38. See Appendix D, page 134, for a reproducible.) Students can either use the graphic organizer or they can list the same information on sticky notes and place them on the textbook page. (See Figure 2.5.) By actively surveying the information in the section, the students are identifying and using the text features to help them comprehend the material they are reading. They are using the text features to determine which information may be more important than other information. (If the information is repeated or highlighted in a text box, it is usually an important point to know.) Last, they are summarizing key points by identifying big ideas in short phrases and vocabulary that appears in the text.

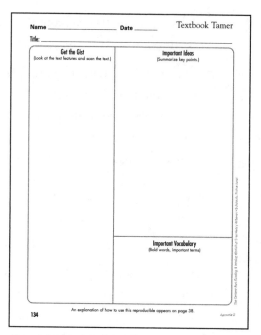

Figure 2.4: Textbook Tamer graphic organizer

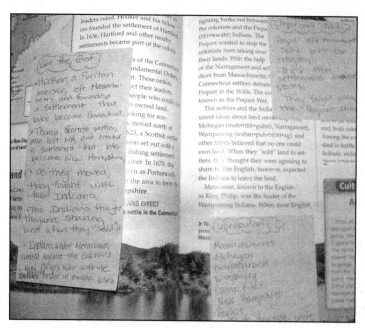

Figure 2.5: Sticky notes on textbook page

Text survey process:

1. Identify the basic, important information listed in headings, graphics, and bold words.

2. Write that information in the "Get the Gist" box on the organizer.

3. List vocabulary words that appear to be important.

4. Identify important ideas (each section usually has two or three) and write two or more bullet points to quickly describe each.

The Content-Rich Reading & Writing Workshop

Leveled Nonfiction/Content Book Reading

Students often dive into reading all nonfiction texts in the same manner, even though these texts may differ greatly in how they present information. Children need to become savvy readers and consumers of nonfiction materials. Because many struggling readers can decode the text but are unable to organize information presented in text or recall details, they need an organizer to help them focus on main ideas and supporting details (Arthaud & Goracke, 2006). Students who are on grade level also need help to organize information, as they are often reading nonfiction texts, leveled texts or magazines, and research information independently. Using a structured outline strategy can help students understand information presented in a variety of materials whether or not the text level is a perfect match for them.

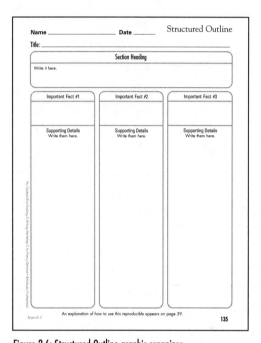

Figure 2.6: Structured Outline graphic organizer

Figure 2.6 provides an example of a Structured Outline graphic organizer designed to help students recall details and facts. The student writes the section heading at the top of the page. Below that, there's a column for each important fact. The student lists the fact at the top of the column and the supporting details for the fact below it. (See Appendix E, page 135, for a reproducible.)

Structured Outline of a Nonfiction Chapter Book

Nonfiction chapter books are often dense with information. It can be difficult for students to understand the important facts in each chapter and the ways in which the facts build from chapter to chapter. While these texts may look like novels, and often have narrative sections, they don't deliver information in a story format. When using the structured outline with texts like these, have students identify three main points in each chapter and fill in the supporting details.

Look at the structure of this short passage from the book *The Pharaohs of Ancient Egypt*, a Landmark Book by Elizabeth Payne (1964).

> *Once he had set up his own headquarters in captured Cairo, Napoleon established the Egyptian Institute as headquarters for his scholars. They were soon hard at work on their various projects. Of them all, the French artist Dominique-Vivant Denon had the most exciting adventures in the months that followed. For when the defeated Egyptian cavalry galloped off into the desert to regroup its forces, Napoleon sent part of his army chasing after them. Denon went along as the representative of the Egyptian Institute.*
>
> *As the French army followed its quarry deeper and deeper into Egypt, Denon began to have the eerie feeling that he was traveling straight into the past.*

Now, keep in mind that this is just a snippet of a 16-page chapter in a 180-page book. If a child misses the point that the chapter is focusing on (which is how Napoleon's army brought to light information about one of the world's greatest civilizations), he may have trouble discerning interesting information from important facts and details.

Figure 2.7 provides an example of a structured outline for Chapter 1 of *The Pharaohs of Ancient Egypt*. If you're working with students ready to read dense texts like this on their own, you can monitor their thinking and comprehension by meeting with them and discussing what they think the main ideas of the chapter includes, and by having them discuss supporting details in paired groups.

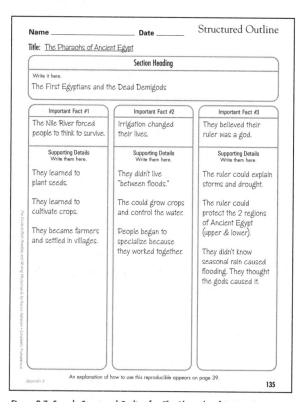

Figure 2.7: Sample Structured Outline for *The Pharaohs of Ancient Egypt*

Structured Outline of a Leveled Nonfiction Text

Completing a structured outline for a leveled nonfiction text is easier, as these texts tend to organize information presented in each section by using bold words, text boxes, diagrams, and illustrations. Figures 2.8 and 2.9 show text from *Wetlands* by Darlene R. Stille (1999) and an example of a Structured Outline for it. This book has about one paragraph per page, in a large font. Each picture includes a caption highlighted in a large box with print offset in an eye-catching color. Children can use the text, the picture, and the caption to reinforce the main ideas and details they pull out from text.

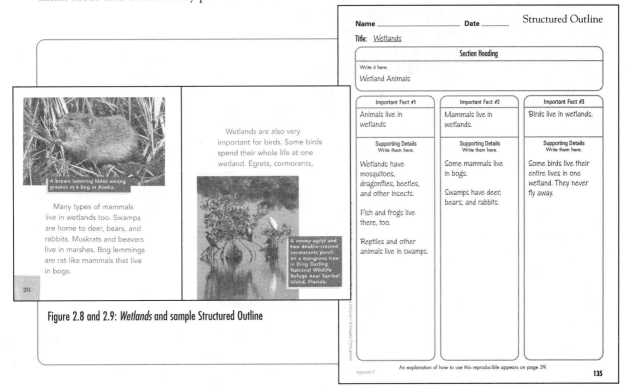

Figure 2.8 and 2.9: *Wetlands* and sample Structured Outline

Structured Outline of a Nonfiction Magazine Article

The magazine article provides yet a different way for students to relate to and comprehend text. Magazines such as Scholastic's *Scope* focus on a feature idea and grab children's attention with photos, graphics, color-coded boxes, captions, and bold words. Short articles like the one on page 42, "Voices of Freedom," may include less information than what students encounter in library books, online resources, or textbooks. This article is conveniently divided into three main points, and each of the three text boxes lists key information on one person and his or her involvement in the civil rights movement. This text is student-friendly and works well as a fluency builder. Students can take turns reading the text to one another and then complete the structured outline together. Remember that if you choose to use this type of text for fluency practice, allow students time to read the section on their own first. (See Figures 2.10 and 2.11.)

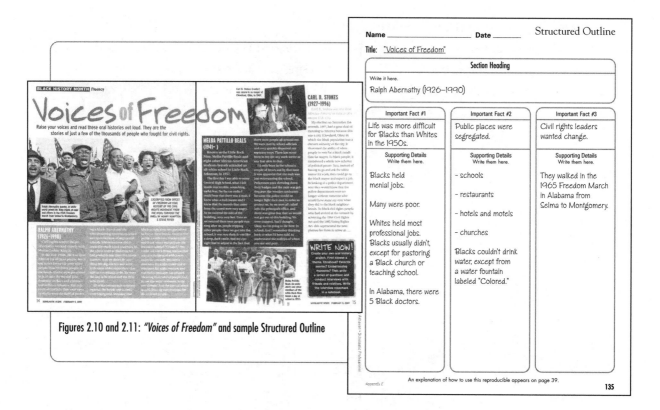

Figures 2.10 and 2.11: *"Voices of Freedom"* and sample Structured Outline

▶ **Buoy Students' Efforts**

Give students floaters by

◆ ensuring they read nonfiction or expository text every day.

◆ teaching them to "tame" the text by scanning and skimming text *before* reading.

◆ teaching them tools to remember what they read.

▶ **Reading Instruction Is Active**

◆ Coach your students while reading.

◆ Remind them of their goals.

◆ Remind them of strategies that work.

◆ Prod them to apply themselves while giving encouragement.

◆ Structure note: The teacher is moving about the room unless meeting with a small group.

CHAPTER 3

Teach the Fundamental Five

Comprehension Strategies That Support Lifelong Learning

In the previous chapters we laid the groundwork for content-rich reading workshops through the use of strategies such as these:

- Setting purposes and goals for reading

- Introducing common structures used to organize informational text

- Activating and developing content knowledge by making connections

Before we move into the fundamental five—strategies that help students become powerful readers in all content areas—it's important to understand the relationship between learning and memory as well as the role the brain plays in storing and retrieving information.

Learning and Memory

Have you ever had the experience of trying to remember something, but your memory is fuzzy and somewhat out of focus? You know it, and yet you just can't grasp the idea out of your brain and present it in a way that makes sense to anyone else? In these instances, a neurologist would tell you that you don't yet have a well-traveled "brain map." There is a path connecting to the new information or idea you learned, but when you try to recall the information, the words and ideas come out jumbled.

Let's take a look at the brain and see how it relates to the challenge of learning and memory. To simplify a very complex subject, our brain is a web of interconnected cells. In fact, there are about a trillion cells in our brains (Sousa, 2006). Nerve cells called neurons are one type of brain cell. They are different from other cells in our bodies in that they have the ability to transmit information. They communicate with other neurons through electrical and chemical signals (Sousa, 2006; Wolfe, 2001; Zull, 2002). Although neurons come in different shapes, their structure remains relatively constant.

Neurons are composed of a cell body (soma), which contains the nucleus. Projecting from the soma are tens of thousands of branches called dendrites. Dendrites receive information via electrical impulses from other neurons and transmit the information down a long fiber, called an axon. The electrical impulses travel down the axon and are transmitted via chemicals called neurotransmitters to other neurons in the synapse, a small gap between the cells (Lyons, 2003; Sousa, 2006; Wolfe 2001).

When we learn, there is a physical change in our brains. Learning creates new experiences for us, and research shows that new experiences change the wiring in our brains. New dendrites form when our brains are stimulated with new information and this information is reinforced and repeated. When dendrites grow, neurons become more complex, creating more synapses and more ways our brain can store and retrieve information (Zull, 2002).

Information is stored and retrieved along neural pathways that fire together. What is stored and retrieved depends on how the neurons grow and how the dendrites fire. When we are presented with new information that we don't understand, or that doesn't connect to anything we already now, it washes away and isn't stored in our memory. If we can *wire* new information to something we already know, it is more likely that the information will be stored and remembered. A very simple way of thinking of this phenomenon is *what wires together, fires together* (Zull, 2002). The information and concepts we organize and learn (wire), we can retrieve more easily (fire). Comprehension and content learning strategies have the potential to help students grow dendrites and to organize and store information.

The Fundamental Five: Focus on Comprehension

Comprehension consists of understanding what you read, whereas memory involves being able to learn and recall information. Research has validated a small number of strategies that improve both comprehension and memory of text for students in upper elementary grades and in middle school. These strategies are the fundamental five that will focus your teaching (Brown, 2002; Pressley, 2002a).

The Fundamental Five Strategies

1. Relating text to background knowledge

2. Understanding and using text structure

3. Asking questions while reading

4. Creating mental images of content

5. Summarizing

Students need as much practice putting information into their brains as pulling information out of their brains. The three keys to using strategies are *connect*, *map*, and *remember*. In order to learn content, students must do all of the following:

■ Connect information

■ Create road maps in their brains to learn the information

■ Remember information by recalling it when needed

Students connect, map, and remember by thinking about texts over and over to answer the questions they generate while reading.

There are simple ways to practice recall through structured engagement activities. You structure these activities so *all* students participate and *bring the information back up through their mental road maps*. All students then practice responding orally or in writing in order to remember with clarity. This is simply a spiral review. In a spiral review we hear new information, map it, and review it often. Then we travel the mental road map to retrieve the information many times to practice *recalling* the new learning.

1. Relating Text to Background Knowledge

Research shows that comprehension improves when students link information presented in reading with knowledge they already possess (Brown, 2002; Pressley, 2002b, 2004). Think of the neural pathways in our brains, where information is linked together by networks of cells that fire together to store and recall information. Remember, what wires together, fires together. So, the goal of teaching students the strategy of relating text to background knowledge is to get them to *wire* new information to something they already know to help them understand and recall content from texts.

Connecting text to prior knowledge has two aspects:

Making predictions: When students make predictions about what they are reading, they form a hypothesis about what they think the text is going to say or show them. Then, while reading, they stop from time to time and reflect on their predictions to see if they were right or wrong.

Forming associations based on previous experiences: By associating ideas and information, students can understand what they read, and increase their chances of remembering the new information. For instance, a student may have knowledge about plant structure, so in fifth grade, when learning about plant cell structure, she can connect the cell structure to her knowledge of what plants need. If a student knows that plants get food from the sun through photosynthesis, learning that plant cells have mitochondria to store food makes sense, and she can connect those ideas together. She might also connect the idea of mitochondria's role as storage cells to the plastic containers her mom uses to store leftovers in the fridge.

Using Concept Maps to Link Information

Concept maps are an effective way to link abstract ideas and reinforce the associations between text and previously developed knowledge. Concept maps also are excellent ways to organize new information to make it easier to learn. Don't limit the use of such maps to reading. They can be used to help students organize and store information from a lecture, interview, video, or other information source. Concept maps help students become active learners (Akhavan, 2006).

You can begin using concept maps by having students connect to ideas through talking and thinking (Wolfe, 2001). After discussing relationships between concepts and known information, record the ideas together on a class map. As students become proficient at mapping, they can fill out individual sheets and save them in a binder or folder. Some concept maps are also known as semantic maps. Semantic maps are used to relate vocabulary terms and teach the meanings and differences between words and the concepts they represent.

Concept mapping consists of two steps (Sousa, 2006):

1. Extracting ideas, information, and terms from content

2. Plotting the information visually to show and define the relationships among the concepts

Concept maps help students visualize content that they may not have understood as they were reading it, or as it was presented to them orally. There are dozens of concept maps, also known as graphic organizers, available to use when learning information.

- Web maps illustrate classification and show similarity and difference in relationships.

- Hierarchy maps depict order and ranking relationships.

- Sequence maps show timelines, steps in a process, and order of use.

- Analogy maps illustrate similarities between concepts. These maps include Venn diagrams, which also reflect differences.

- Plot maps represent story structure and informational text structure.

Several concepts maps are included in the Appendix, including a plot map, sequence map, hierarchy map, and analogy map. Again, these maps reinforce the strategy you are teaching by making both the strategy and the new information visual.

For example, notice how information is portrayed visually on page 47. (See Figures 3.1 and 3.2.) This is an example of a web map for the vocabulary words presented in the *Super Science* article, "Going the Distance." In the article, six content words are identified and defined. The words "red crab" are written in the circle in the middle of the web. The other circles show the terms defined in the article. The additional notes written around the edges of the circles are the connections the student made to his prior knowledge about the vocabulary words. (See Appendix F, page 136, for a reproducible.)

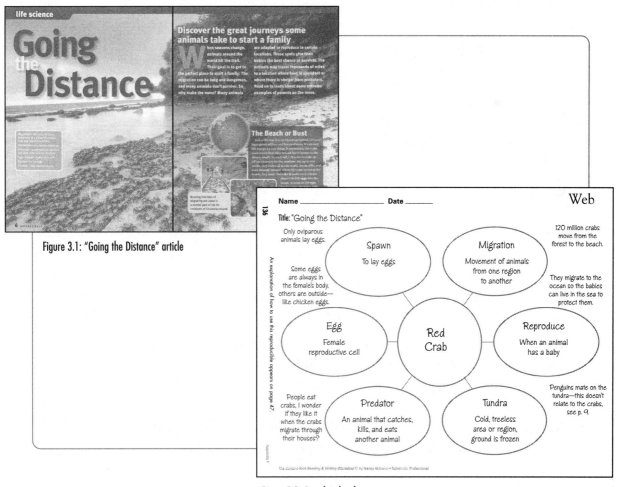

Figure 3.1: "Going the Distance" article

Figure 3.2: Completed web

Making Connections—Analogies That Work

Probably the most familiar way to help students relate text to background knowledge is by teaching them how to make connections. There are three basic types of connections students make while reading:

- Text-to-self connections
- Text-to-text connections
- Text-to-world connections

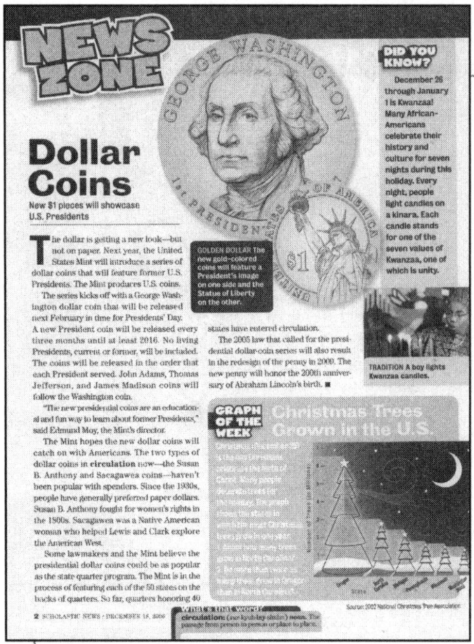

NEWS ZONE

Dollar Coins

New $1 pieces will showcase U.S. Presidents

The dollar is getting a new look—but not on paper. Next year, the United States Mint will introduce a series of dollar coins that will feature former U.S. Presidents. The Mint produces U.S. coins.

The series kicks off with a George Washington dollar coin that will be released next February in time for Presidents' Day. A new President coin will be released every three months until at least 2016. No living Presidents, current or former, will be included. The coins will be released in the order that each President served. John Adams, Thomas Jefferson, and James Madison coins will follow the Washington coin.

"The new presidential coins are an educational and fun way to learn about former Presidents," said Edmund Moy, the Mint's director.

The Mint hopes the new dollar coins will catch on with Americans. The two types of dollar coins in **circulation** now—the Susan B. Anthony and Sacagawea coins—haven't been popular with spenders. Since the 1930s, people have generally preferred paper dollars. Susan B. Anthony fought for women's rights in the 1800s. Sacagawea was a Native American woman who helped Lewis and Clark explore the American West.

Some lawmakers and the Mint believe the presidential dollar coins could be as popular as the state quarter program. The Mint is in the process of featuring each of the 50 states on the backs of quarters. So far, quarters honoring 40 states have entered circulation.

The 2005 law that called for the presidential dollar-coin series will also result in the redesign of the penny in 2009. The new penny will honor the 200th anniversary of Abraham Lincoln's birth. ■

GOLDEN DOLLAR The new gold-colored coins will feature a President's image on one side and the Statue of Liberty on the other.

DID YOU KNOW?

December 26 through January 1 is Kwanzaa! Many African-Americans celebrate their history and culture for seven nights during this holiday. Every night, people light candles on a kinara. Each candle stands for one of the seven values of Kwanzaa, one of which is unity.

TRADITION A boy lights Kwanzaa candles.

GRAPH OF THE WEEK Christmas Trees Grown in the U.S.

Source: 2002 National Christmas Tree Association

circulation (sur-kyuh-lay-shuhn) **noun.** The passage from person to person or place to place.

2 SCHOLASTIC NEWS / DECEMBER 18, 2006

Figure 3.3: "Dollar Coins" article

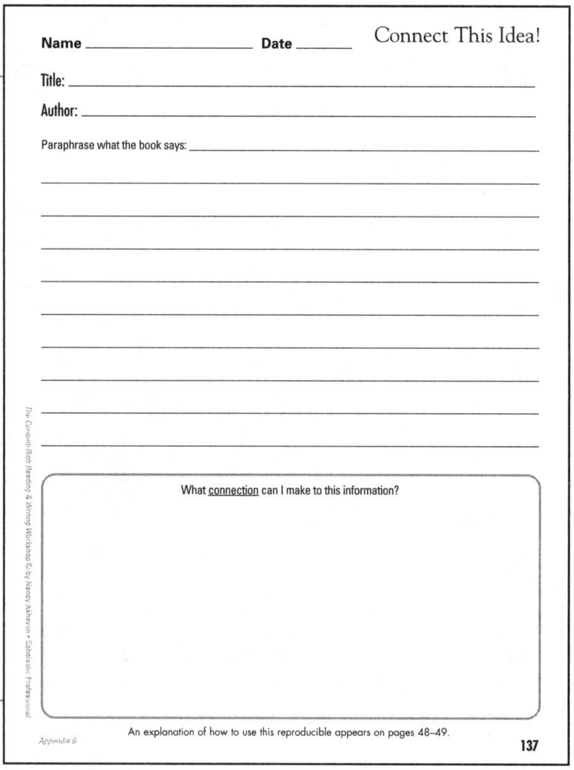

Name ____________ Date ______ Connect This Idea!

Title: ____________

Author: ____________

Paraphrase what the book says: ____________

What connection can I make to this information?

An explanation of how to use this reproducible appears on pages 48–49.

137

The Content-Rich Reading & Writing Workshop by Nancy Akhavan • Scholastic Professional

Figure 3.4 Connect This Idea! sheet

Making connections is a way for students to make analogies between prior knowledge and new information. Students gather knowledge in different ways, including through personal experience, concepts learned in a book or other text, and information they know. The key to teaching students to make such analogies is to first make sure that they are identifying and connecting what they read and then that they are identifying and connecting information in their reading to prior knowledge. Often when I am working with a group of students who know they need to make a connection to the text, they choose to connect to the unimportant and trivial details. Students need to make connections between the big ideas in the text and their prior knowledge.

Take a look at the article "Dollar Coins" from *Scholastic News*. (See Figure 3.3.) If a student connects to the big ideas in this text, he might mention that he collects the commemorative state quarters, or that the image on the coin resembles the image on the dollar bill. These are excellent connections to the text. If a student says, "Once I found a quarter in the parking lot" or "my parents had an anniversary too," he clearly would be making superficial connections to the text that do not help him learn as effectively as deep connections.

Students can write their connections in a reading response journal. Connect This Idea! is a process for students to follow *while* reading to encourage them to make connections to text.

(See Figure 3.4 on page 48.) First, have the students read a portion of text, reviewing illustrations, important words, and text features as they go. Then ask students to describe anything they know that the text or the text features reminds them of. Finally, tell students to paraphrase what they've read, and then write about their connection. The process of paraphrasing the information from the text becomes a cue to wake up students' brains and will help them recall the new information later. It may help to have them share their paraphrase and connection orally with partners first. (See Appendix G, page 137, for a reproducible.) By writing their connection down alongside the paraphrased text, new concepts and learning are reinforced (Sousa, 2006).

2. Understanding and Using Text Structure

By the time they enter fourth grade, students come to our classrooms with an understanding of "story." They are able to comprehend stories and retell story elements with ease, due to their familiarity with the narrative text structure. Students don't come to our upper-grade classrooms as prepared to read informational texts. In essence, they don't have a mental road map in their heads (Ogle & Blachowicz, 2002). As students learn, they develop a coherent and usable mental representation of text (Lyons, 2003; Stein & Glenn, 1979). This mental representation is similar to a network. Neurons and their thousands of dendrites (each neuron can have as a many as 100,000 dendrites) intertwine in all directions to form a connected tangle (Lyons, 2003). Remember that, in simple terms, learning occurs when neural pathways become stronger and easier to fire. The stronger the path is, the more automatic the processing (Sousa, 2006). Once again, it helps to remember that "what wires together, fires together".

When students unfamiliar with informational text survey or scan the text prior to reading, they don't have a well-established path in their brains for understanding its structure. To provide them with the knowledge they need to read and comprehend informational text, we need to help them develop a mental road map. That requires many, many experiences with informational texts in order to understand the common structures used to organize these types of texts. We can help them learn about text structure by calling attention to the features that organize different types of informational text. Not only will students be able to grasp the main idea more quickly once they understand text structure, their road map will also help them keep track of the most important information (Block, Schaller, Joy, & Gaine, 2002; Brown, 2002;. (See Chapter 1, pp. 19–25, for more information on text structure.)

Text Feature Sheet

It is important for students to familiarize themselves with the text features of informational materials *before* they begin reading. Be specific in helping students use informational texts, as they may not have the experience to know how the text features help them comprehend and learn. Teach students the strategy of looking at text features through a Text Feature Sheet. Before reading, a student would identify the title and author, a few text features (diagrams, index, pictures), and two or three points that the text features suggest are important. When students examine text features before reading, they are waking up their brains by recalling what text features do and how the features organize information. The Text Feature Sheet also wakes up the brain by having a student notice two or three ideas that she will be reading about. This simple way of focusing helps a student remember anything she might know about the subject or concept and stimulates her brain to take in new information.

The completed Text Feature Sheet is based on the book *Our Earth* by Kenneth Walsh (2004). (See Figures 3.5 and 3.6.) It lists concepts that a student might learn while looking at the diagram on page 19. The book, written at a reading level of grade 2.6, would be an excellent type of text to use with a student reading below grade level.

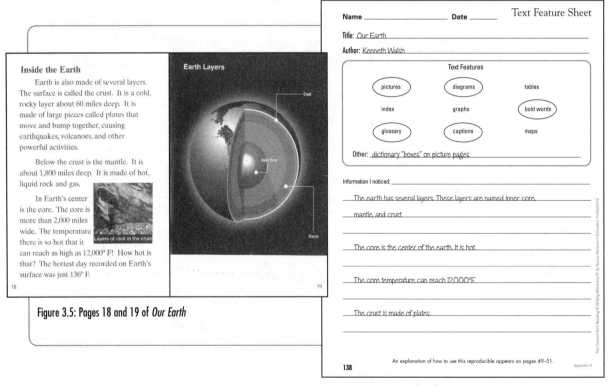

Figure 3.5: Pages 18 and 19 of *Our Earth*

Figure 3.6: Text Feature Sheet for *Our Earth*

Another example of a Text Feature Sheet, based on the book *Secrets of the Sphinx* by James Giblin (2004), appears on page 51. (See Figures 3.7 and 3.8). This informational picture book, written at a reading level for upper elementary students, would be appropriate for students at or above grade level. The Text Feature Sheet can be used for students reading a variety of material at a variety of reading levels. (See Appendix H, page 138, for a reproducible.)

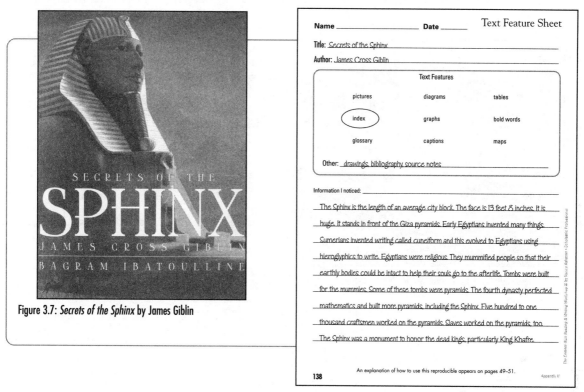

Figure 3.7: *Secrets of the Sphinx* by James Giblin

Figure 3.8 Completed Text Feature Sheet for *Secrets of the Sphinx*

Problem-Solution Sheet

Many informational texts are organized in a problem-solution format. The Problem-Solution sheet focuses students on connecting main ideas with supporting events and related information. In most texts there is at least one main idea presented for the problem and at least one main idea presented for the solution. Simpler texts tend to focus on a single main idea or concept with several supporting details. More sophisticated texts may present more than one idea or concept for a problem or solution. The Problem-Solution sheet is designed for students to identify one main idea/concept and to list supporting facts below the main idea. Students then write the solution presented in the text.

The lines and the circle on this graphic organizer are designed to help students visualize the problem and the solution and see that text can be represented graphically to help them comprehend and remember. See the visualization strategy section, pp. 54–56, for a description of this process.

An example of the map filled out for the article "Fuel for Thought" from *Scholastic Scope* appears below. (See Figures 3.9 and 3.10.) This article outlines how rising oil prices have caused schools to cut back on field trips due to high fuel costs. The end of the article outlines a few ideas about how students can help reduce fuel usage. (See Appendix I, page 139, for a reproducible.)

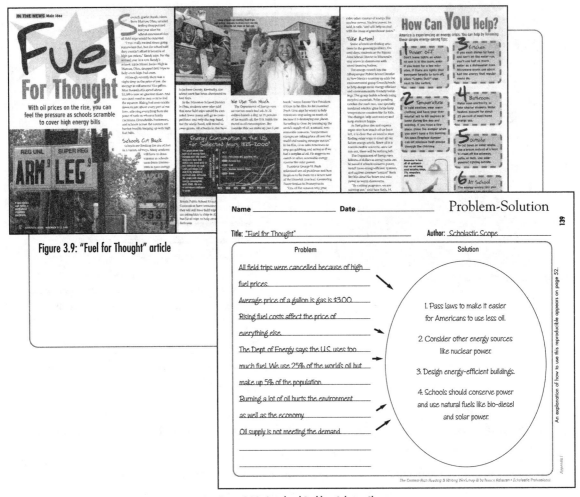

Figure 3.9: "Fuel for Thought" article

Figure 3.10: Completed Problem-Solution Sheet

Identifying Important information Sheet

Many informational texts use a descriptive text structure. Within the description, there is a hierarchy to the ideas presented. Some information and ideas are more important than others. Students need lots and lots of practice with a variety of texts to become proficient at identifying the most important information when reading. One great way to teach students to identify a hierarchal structure in text is to give them two or three highlighter pens of different colors. As you read a text out loud, have your students highlight two or three important ideas, using a different color for each one. In the beginning you will need to walk students through this activity, telling them what is important as they probably won't have the skills to identify the relative importance of one fact over another.

When your students are ready to record their thinking, use the Identifying Important Information sheet (see Figure 3.11). This sheet helps students clearly identify important facts from a body of information they have collected. Students list facts that were in the text; then they pull out two or three important facts. Listing facts they identified while reading, rechecking the text, and then selecting the most important ideas helps students learn to sift through information in descriptive texts. The sheet also has a place to list important vocabulary words from the text. (See Appendix J, page 140, for a reproducible.)

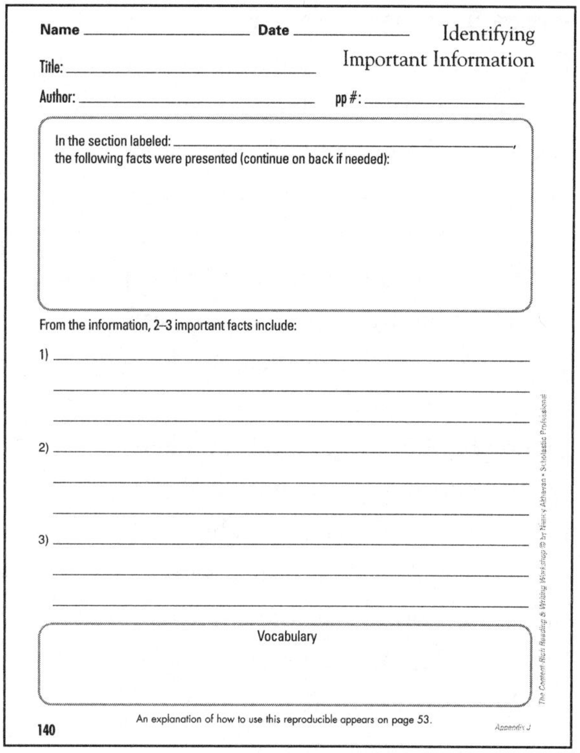

Name ____________ Date ____________ Identifying Important Information

Title: ____________

Author: ____________ pp #: ____________

In the section labeled: ____________,
the following facts were presented (continue on back if needed):

From the information, 2–3 important facts include:

1) ____________

2) ____________

3) ____________

Vocabulary

140

An explanation of how to use this reproducible appears on page 53.

Appendix J

The Content-Rich Reading & Writing Workshop © by Nancy Akhavan • Scholastic Professional

Figure 3.11: Identifying Important Information Sheet

3. Asking Questions While Reading

This strategy is tricky, but it immensely helps students comprehend informational texts. Asking questions while reading is tricky because a student who doesn't comprehend what he has read might not ask any questions at all. Yes, we *assume* he might ask, "Why don't I get this?" But this doesn't always happen, so focusing on questioning teaches students to become active and involved with reading and their own learning.

When students learn to ask questions of themselves before, during, and after reading, their comprehension improves. By asking questions prior to reading a text, students are learning to wake up their brains and tap prior knowledge on a subject. When they ask *who, what,* and *when* questions while reading, they are identifying literal information in a text (Brown, 2002). *Why* questions help students process that information at a deeper level. When answering *why* questions, students integrate information within the text and go beyond it. As students connect information within the text, they are connecting and mapping information, and as they connect information to background knowledge, they are growing new road maps in their brains.

Asking Questions Bookmark

One way to encourage students to ask questions *while* reading is to give them an Asking Questions Bookmark. Now, this bookmark does mark their place in a text, but more importantly, students write on the bookmark to help them focus on the steps in the process. The bookmark reminds them to (1) pause and ask themselves, "Do I know what I just read?" and (2) ask a question, focusing on literal recall of what they read, such as "What was this section about?" or "What details did the section give about the main idea?" See Figure 3.12 for an example of a bookmarks page. (See Appendix K, page 141, for a reproducible.)

Asking Questions Bookmark		
PAUSE & CHECK	**PAUSE & CHECK**	**PAUSE & CHECK**
Step 1) Ask yourself: "Do I understand what I just read?" If you answered yes: Keep reading If you answered no: Reread the section	Step 1) Ask yourself: "Do I understand what I just read?" If you answered yes: Keep reading If you answered no: Reread the section	Step 1) Ask yourself: "Do I understand what I just read?" If you answered yes: Keep reading If you answered no: Reread the section
Step 2) If you understand what you read, then ask yourself: "What is this section or page about?" (Describe it to yourself.) AND "What details support the main idea?" (List them in your head.) AND When did this occur?" (Check the dates/time/period in history.)	Step 2) If you understand what you read, then ask yourself: "What is this section or page about?" (Describe it to yourself.) AND "What details support the main idea?" (List them in your head.) AND When did this occur?" (Check the dates/time/period in history.)	Step 2) If you understand what you read, then ask yourself: "What is this section or page about?" (Describe it to yourself.) AND "What details support the main idea?" (List them in your head.) AND When did this occur?" (Check the dates/time/period in history.)
Step 3) Now, tell yourself the gist of the section. **Keep reading!**	Step 3) Now, tell yourself the gist of the section. **Keep reading!**	Step 3) Now, tell yourself the gist of the section. **Keep reading!**

Cut the bookmarks apart. Have students use a bookmark while reading to aid comprehension.

Appendix K   An explanation of how to use this reproducible appears on page 54.   **141**

Figure 3.12: Asking Questions Bookmark

4. Creating Mental Images of Content

It is important to deal with concepts visually as well as verbally. We often forget to help students visualize what we teach. Visualization doesn't always mean we develop a picture in our minds; it is just as effective to visualize new concepts with figures, lines, dots, and other geometric shapes. Any visual image helps students map new concepts and remember them (Zull, 2002). For example, last week I taught my daughter the steps to making a particular Persian dish we eat often at home. As I thought of how to help her learn that cooking almost all Persian main dishes begins in a similar way, I realized that there was a pattern to cooking a number of dishes I could teach her: cut the onion, fry it with spices, add meat, add vegetables, add lemon juice and water, simmer for a long time. Now, this is a simple framework, but my goal was to teach her a few basic steps that she could use to cook several different dishes. My visual for these steps looks like this:

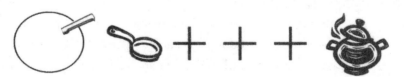

Figure 3.13: Visual representation of cooking steps

When students can construct an image of what they read, the image becomes a representation of the text and helps them remember what they read (Trabasso & Bouchard, 2002; Zull 2002). Visualization is a skill that develops over time, and obviously, it is best taught with highly descriptive texts or with information that can be displayed graphically. What we visualize becomes a mnemonic device to remember what was read. If students are reading about photosynthesis, and they visualize arrows (—➤) pointing at the leaves and minus symbols (–) surrounding the leaves, they can visualize how the plant turns sunlight into food and releases carbon dioxide.

Help students grasp new concepts by teaching them to see pictures in their minds. Do this through sketching, and adding arrows, boxes, and other geometric shapes to sketches to show concepts, or by creating graphics to represent information, including steps in a process, progression over time, or parts of an idea.

Picture It! Sheet

The Picture It! sheet helps students focus on what they see in their minds after reading a section of the text. The sheet can be used for the beginning, middle, or end of the text. The stoplight

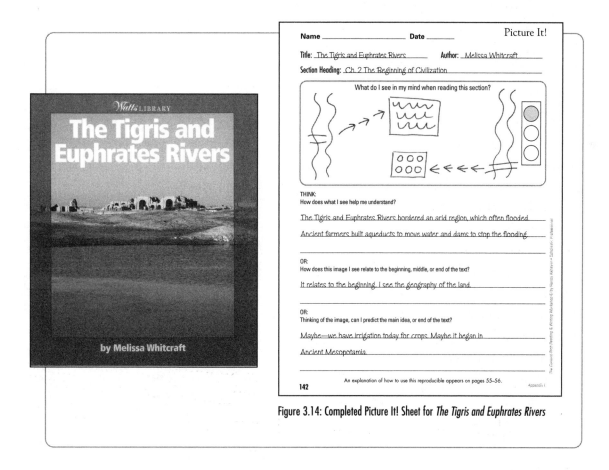

Figure 3.14: Completed Picture It! Sheet for *The Tigris and Euphrates Rivers*

picture on the right side of the box is a mnemonic to help students focus on beginning, middle, and end. If students draw a picture or diagram from the beginning of a text, have them darken the top circle. For the middle of the text, have them darken the middle circle, and for the end, have them darken the bottom circle. (See Figure 3.14 for an example.)

By organizing the visualization process in this manner, students can develop an understanding of text structure as well as focus on understanding the content by *seeing* what they've read. It is very likely that you'll want students to use more than one sheet for concepts presented in the middle of the text. After reading a short text, students might have a stack of four or five papers: one recording their visualization from the beginning of the text, two or three representing the middle, and one representing the end. The Picture It! sheets not only help students comprehend what they are reading but also help them map new information in their brains. (See Appendix L, page 142, for a reproducible.)

5. Summarizing

When students summarize, they are more aware of how text is structured and how ideas relate to each other (Trabasso & Bouchard, 2002). They learn to identify important ideas, generalize information, and minimize details. Teaching students to restate in their own words what they've read encourages them to stop, think, and recall. It is also a simple and fast way for you to assess a student's ability to read a particular text and grasp the main idea.

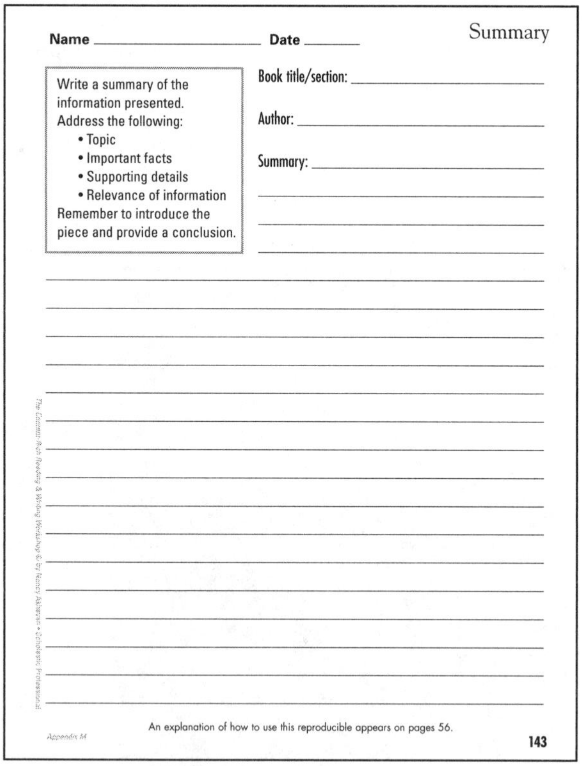
Name ____ Date ____ Summary

Write a summary of the information presented. Address the following:
- Topic
- Important facts
- Supporting details
- Relevance of information

Remember to introduce the piece and provide a conclusion.

Book title/section: ____

Author: ____

Summary: ____

The Content-Rich Reading & Writing Workshop © by Nancy Akhavan • Scholastic Professional

Appendix M

An explanation of how to use this reproducible appears on pages 56.

143

Figure 3.15: Summary sheet

Summarization goes beyond teaching students to determine importance in text. When students determine importance in text, they are asking themselves questions to determine *what they find to be most critical to know and remember*.

Summarization, on the other hand, requires students to sift through a larger piece of text, differentiate information for importance, and then synthesize the ideas into a new text that is coherent and represents the original text

(Dole, Duffy, Roehler, & Pearson, 1991; Duke & Pearson, 2002). Does this sound difficult? It is.

As a reading strategy, summarization is a self-review activity. Students monitor their own progress by thinking succinctly, "What did I read?" and "What does it mean?" We can teach students to stop reading and ask themselves or one another to do the following:

- State what just happened in the text.

- Think of a synopsis.

There are two basic ways to teach summarization. One is by having students follow a protocol, or expected framework. The other is by teaching students to understand the gist of the text and write their thoughts in an informal summary (Pearson & Duke, 2002). When we teach students to use a framework to write summaries, we focus them on following protocols to prioritize information, exclude extraneous details, and synthesize ideas in their own words. When we ask students to discuss orally a summary of what they have read, or ask them to jot down a quick summary in a notebook, this is generally a free recall task, and students will give us the gist of what they have read (Stahl, 2006). (See Figure 3.15 on page 56 for an example of a Summary sheet. A reproducible can be found in Appendix M on page 143.) When students use this frame, they identify what they read, by whom, and what section, if applicable. Then they write about these topics and concepts from the text based on the prompts.

Information Frame

This framework for teaching students to summarize focuses them on the processes that help them identify information and then rethink it succinctly (Pearson & Duke, 2002; Trabasso & Bouchard, 2002). These processes include the following:

- Identifying the main idea

- Deleting redundant material

- Choosing a word or phrase to replace a list of items

- Choosing a word or phrase to replace actions or events

- Creating a topic sentence

Figure 3.16: Information Frame

Teach students the steps in the process by practicing in a large group, reading a text out loud, and then filling in the Information Frame together. (See Figure 3.16 for an example of an Information Frame.) Have students complete frames individually from their own reading of an informational text. (See Appendix N, page 144, for a reproducible.)

Reading Response Frame

Summarization requires students to attend to and think about the text in a specific way. This strategy gives them a structure to follow. (See Figure 3.17 for an example of one type of Reading Response frame. A reproducible can be found in Appendix O, page 145.) When students use this frame, they identify what they read, by whom, and focus on the beginning, middle, or end of the text. They write about the gist of the text.

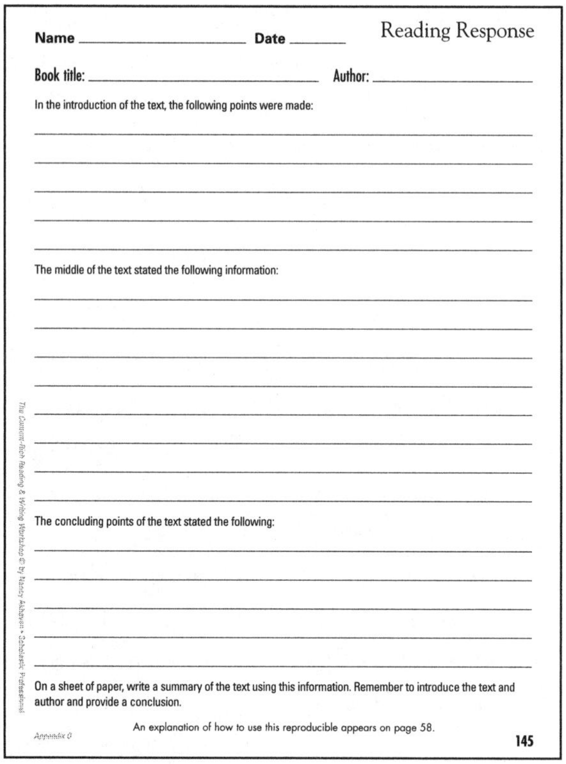
Name ________ Date ______ Reading Response

Book title: ________ Author: ________

In the introduction of the text, the following points were made:

The middle of the text stated the following information:

The concluding points of the text stated the following:

On a sheet of paper, write a summary of the text using this information. Remember to introduce the text and author and provide a conclusion.

An explanation of how to use this reproducible appears on page 58.

Appendix O 145

The Content-Rich Reading & Writing Workshop © by Nancy Akhavan • Scholastic Professional

Figure 3.17: Reading Response Frame

When students write, they are taking time to reflect on their reading and new learning, organize concepts, and remember new information. The goal of writing a reading response is to transfer new information from short-term or working memory to long-term memory so students can learn and recall new concepts. Journal writing has been proven to be a highly effectively strategy for transfer (Sousa, 2006; Zull, 2002). Assembling language helps students take new ideas that are forming in their brains and organize it to share it and learn it. When students tell other people about new ideas, they are connecting their new learning to prior knowledge and new neural pathways are being formed and reinforced (Zull, 2002). Similarly, when students write about and summarize their reading, their brains are working to make those connections as they assemble language to tell about what they have read or learned (Knipper & Duggan, 2006).

Reading response frames don't have to be fancy; in fact, all your students need is a blank notebook and an organized way to write about what they have read. It is preferable to use a consistent framework in your class. Research has shown that using a protocol for students to think, recall, and write is more effective than unstructured response (Tierney & Cunningham, 2002).

Two-Column Note Taking

Note taking is a time-honored method of summarizing ideas and information. In two-column note taking, students focus on critical attributes that make a concept unique (Sousa, 2006). When they focus on attributes, they can remember and retrieve information.

Teach students to organize their thinking in two columns *during* and *after* reading a selection. By thinking about what they read, and rereading to focus on selected information, students will have a greater chance of comprehending the text and remembering information from it. The focus of their thinking, and therefore the column headings, can change, depending on what you want students to learn and how the text is organized. (The appendix contains two-column note organizers for similarities and differences, P: p. 146; main idea and details, Q: p. 147; and gist of the text, R: p. 148.) Teach students to organize a binder or folder to store completed copies of their notes.

Similarities and Differences Organizer

To use this organizer, teach students one concept and list it on the left, and then list a different concept on the right. After students read a selection, discuss similarities and differences between the concepts. Students write these in the appropriate column. (See Figure 3.18.)

When teaching similarities and differences, avoid teaching concepts that are too similar at the same time. Whenever two concepts have more

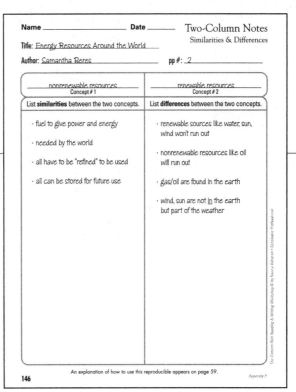

Figure 3.18: Two-Column Notes: Similarities and Differences for
Energy Resources Around the World

similarities than differences (e.g., simile and metaphor), you run the risk that the students won't be able to tell the concepts apart, and they will become confused (Sousa, 2006). In this case, it is better to teach the concepts separately and use a different organizer.

Main Idea and Details Organizer

After you teach students how to use this organizer, they can use it to guide their thinking *while* reading. Tell students to stop at specified places in the text in order to think about what they've read and to identify the main idea of the section. Then students write the main idea they identified. They may copy a sentence or heading if necessary, but it is better for them to mentally walk through the steps of summarization (discussed on p. 57) and think of their own topic sentence, or main idea, of the section. Then students write details that support the main idea. Figure 3.19 is an example of a main idea organizer for the article "The Great Divide" from *Scholastic News*. Notice how each paragraph is summarized in a main idea in the left-hand column and one or two details are jotted down in the right-hand column. (See Figure 3.20.)

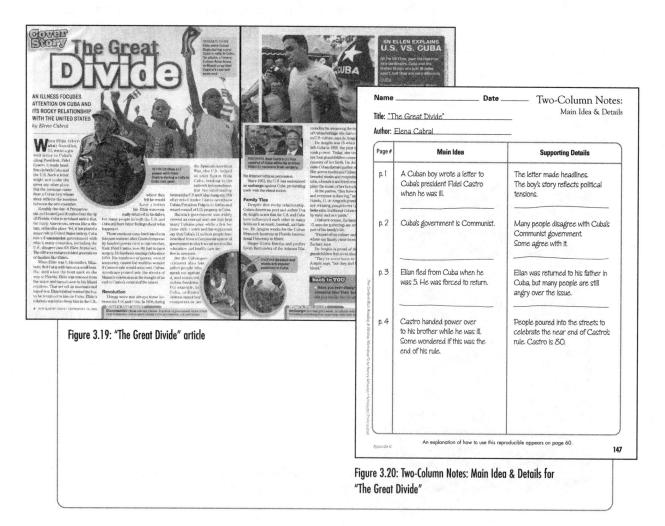

Figure 3.19: "The Great Divide" article

Figure 3.20: Two-Column Notes: Main Idea & Details for "The Great Divide"

Figure 3.21: Two-Column Notes: Get the Gist for *Ellis Island*

The figure shows a reproducible worksheet with the following content:

Two-Column Notes
Get the Gist

Name _____ Date _____

Title: Ellis Island

Author: Patricia Ryon Quiri

Write what the text actually states. Include page numbers.	Write the gist of the text. Jot a note about what you think it is mainly about.
p. 5 "Many questions go through the minds of people who move."	· People may be excited or scared. · It is the unknown.
p. 6 "In the late 1890s and 1900s, many families from Europe needed to move to the U.S."	· America was the land of promise. · People came for a better life.
p. 13 "On Ellis Island, these immigrants had to face questions and medical exams."	· Moving to America wasn't easy. · You couldn't just walk off the boat. · Too many people were coming at once.

148   An explanation of how to use this reproducible appears on page 61.   Appendix B

Gist of the Text Organizer

When you teach students to get the gist of the text, you are teaching them to summarize what they have read so far. *While* reading, the students stop from time to time and think very quickly of one statement that is the gist of what they have read. (A gist note or jot is a one-sentence statement about what was read.) Studies have shown that teaching students to summarize their reading in this way, focusing them on comprehending the text, improves their reading ability (Tierney & Cunningham, 2002).

In a gist organizer, students record a gist statement and corresponding page number (See Figure 3.21.) At first, they may not comprehend the text and may record incorrect information. The point is not for students to learn facts, but to focus on their comprehension by summarizing what they have read.

If students are not recording information correctly, you will know that they are not comprehending it. This organizer not only helps students focus, but it also gives you a quick assessment of their comprehension of a particular text. If students do not comprehend, you will need to focus on teaching fix-up strategies. These include rereading, pausing to think more often, chunking words students do not know how to decode, and writing down words that are unfamiliar so that they can ask for help with word meaning and concepts.

Using the Fundamental Five Strategies to Focus on Learning Content

Remember there are times that you will want students to focus on learning information. Obviously, when they are reading, we want them to comprehend text *and* learn information. But there may be times they are researching and gathering information and not reading. During these times, you will want to teach students how to use the fundamental five strategies to focus on learning content, rather than only focusing on comprehension.

These strategies help struggling readers expand their knowledge base. To help these readers, you may have a partner read difficult texts to them so that they can learn information. As I mentioned in Chapter 2, most textbooks are written about three grade levels above the intended grade level. Struggling readers won't be able to access the content by reading it themselves, so if they listen to it read, or they explore other means to learn the content, they need to know how to use content-learning strategies to remember and recall the information. You might use these strategies when presenting information students cannot access by reading through another medium such as a video clip or oral presentation.

Structured Engagement Strategies to Help Recall

Have you ever taken a test and bombed, but you *knew* that you knew the material going into the test? Perhaps you didn't practice recalling the information enough; maybe you only focused on inputting it into your brain. Recalling information is a different level of knowing and understanding than comprehension. Recall means that you truly learned it; you've gone beyond hearing information, or being familiar with information—with recall you own it.

The activities presented below can help students remember content. Getting up and moving is a key component in each activity. When students get up and move, their brains wake up and blood recirculates in their systems, putting 15 percent more blood in their brains within one minute (Sousa, 2006).

Pair and Talk

The main idea in the pair-and-talk activity is to put novelty into your lesson. Novelty is important to keep students stimulated and engaged. This doesn't mean that you need to jump up and put on an act; it simply means that you need to vary the ways students sit, listen, and interact.

Pair and Talk involves having your students get up and walk to a different part of the room, find a partner, and talk about a concept or idea from the lesson or unit you are teaching. By talking with a partner, they have to practice retrieving newly learned information and putting the concepts back into words in order to express what they know.

Pair and Talk is different from think/pair/share, a common cooperative learning technique. In think/pair/share, students are given the opportunity to think about an idea or concept, take a note or two, and share their thinking with a partner.

The steps in Pair and Talk:

- The teacher asks students to get up and move to another part of the room.

- Each student finds a partner.

- The teacher gives a prompt based on a concept or idea from the lesson or unit.

- Students talk about the ideas and opinions the prompt inspires.

Stand and Deliver

In Stand and Deliver, you call on students to stand, pause (to give time for the blood to move to their brains and wake them up), and deliver information to the group they are working with. Stand and Deliver works well when a small group has information to share with the whole class. It also works well when doing a popcorn share. In a popcorn share, you pose a question to the class regarding a concept or idea, and students *pop* up to discuss it.

Stand and Deliver also works well when students read aloud together, focusing on rereading for fluency or rereading to find facts to complete a strategy sheet. When using Stand and Deliver in this manner, students may work in a small group, standing and filling out a chart on a stand, or reading to one another.

The steps in Stand and Deliver:

- The teacher calls on a student in a group to stand.

- The student stands and, after a short pause, delivers information to the group or whole class orally or by reading.

Take a Stand

This strategy helps students make associations among their emotions, knowledge, and assumptions about a topic. Connecting emotion to any learning is a powerful memory maker! During this activity, students divide up according to their position on an issue. Then during discussion, each side takes turns justifying its position on the subject. One person speaks at a time, while others listen respectfully. Use Take a Stand in the middle or the end of a unit, after students have learned about a topic. Students can refer to their notes and strategy sheets to help them form and state their opinions.

Create a line in the middle of your classroom (it can be a real line made out of tape or an imaginary line represented by classroom furnishings). Pose a question to students regarding an issue related to their informational reading or current unit of study. The question needs to be clear and foster a strong response. For example, from the *Scholastic Scope* article "Fuel for Thought" (see Figure 3.9 on page 52), you could pose a question related to the fuel crunch, for example, *"Is it wrong for schools to cancel field trips or lower the thermostat in winter to reduce fuel bills?"* Then you would ask the students to think for a few moments about which side of the issue they are on. Have students move to one side of the line or the other according to their position. You begin the discussion by throwing a small ball to one side of the line. Whoever catches the ball states his or her opinion and then throws the ball to the other side. The back-and-forth discussion goes on until most students have stated their positions. To close the activity, have students add notes with new information or thoughts to a strategy sheet.

The steps in Take a Stand:

- The teacher poses a question based on informational reading or the current unit of study.

- Students review their notes and think for a few moments about their responses.

- The teacher uses tape or furniture to divide the classroom into two sides.

- Students stand on one side or the other according to their opinion and thoughts about the issue.

- Using a small ball to manage the back-and-forth exchange, the teacher has students state their opinions.

- Students respectfully listen to each speaker.

- After the discussion, students record their current thoughts on the issue and any new information they learned.

On-Ramp to Learning   **Key to Remembering**

- When we can *wire* new information to something we already know, we are more likely to remember it.

- Help children *wire* new information to prior learning through focused, direct instruction.

- *Before* teaching, remind students what they know.
  During teaching, tell them how new learning connects to what they know.
  After teaching, tell them again how the new learning connects to their prior learning.

  What wires together, fires together.

CHAPTER 4

Write Into Knowledge

Straddling the Two Worlds of Writing to Know and Testing to Prove It

Students need to experience and explore writing for a number of purposes within the content-rich workshop:

- To support and develop reading comprehension

- To develop their skills as writers

- To create reports and expository pieces that engage them with content

Overall, students should write often as a way of knowing and processing information. Here are a few types of writing that may occur in content-based workshops:

- Summaries

- Notes—in a binder or notebook and with an organizational tool such as a graphic organizer, or on sticky notes

- Informational reports

- Biographies

- Scientific observations

- Focus booklets (small books filled with notes from a specific chapter or topic)

- Expository pieces

- Persuasive essays

- Procedural reports

Writing Helps Children Learn

Developing their writing abilities is one of the most important gifts you can give children. When children write well, they have an avenue to comprehension and content learning. They also have the tools to create a piece that effectively communicates content in a variety of ways.

Children who write effectively can do the following:

- Convey ideas

- Analyze information

- Persuade and motivate others

- Address a variety of purposes and audiences

- Express their thoughts in unique ways

Learning to write is hard, and it requires that children practice every day. The key is that this practice must be supported by transparent teaching that focuses on two things: pushing the children and telling them, "You *can* do this," and then showing them *how*. The *how* is the tricky part, because if learning to write is difficult, learning to teach writing is just as challenging. Teaching writing is difficult because much of the time, as teachers, we don't write often beyond routine record keeping, or we haven't had the opportunity to write and sometimes we are venturing down a path as learners ourselves.

Just as with reading instruction and content instruction, writing instruction needs to unfold naturally, be clear, and provide responsive feedback to children so they know how to improve their writing. You do this by devoting a block of time every day to writing. You may teach writing during your content time, or you may teach writing in a workshop. Either way, children need focus, explicit guidance, and help, and they need *plenty* of time to simply write.

When children write often to process information, to begin to own information, they write to learn. Even though writing is a ticket to learning, comprehending, and understanding, few teachers actually teach writing. There are a few reasons for that: we teach at breakneck speed, forgetting to slow down and teach things our children don't know how to do, because we have too much to do in a very short amount of time, (to learn how to focus on the speed of learning refer to Chapter 5); we *want* to teach writing, but we run out of time in our busy, busy days (remember to prioritize through an effective planning process; see Chapter 7); and also, we lack confidence in our ability to teach writing (if you weren't taught how to write, it can be intimidating to teach others). So, we resort to *assign and assess.*

The assign-and-assess approach doesn't work when you need to change a student's current level of understanding. The guiding principle of transparent teaching is to *take their hands and show them how.* (See Chapter 7 for more on transparent teaching.) By being clear and by teaching expectations of writing, the art of writing, and the rules of language, we can truly help children open up enough so that we can see their learning *hot spots* and focus on those learning points.

Learning Hot Spots

Writing is a learning hot spot. Few children really know how to write in multiple genres, convey information, and complete an effective essay. The biggest factor contributing to children's lack of writing proficiency is that they don't write very much at all. If children were given the opportunity on a regular basis to write, they would accomplish the following:

- Increase their writing skills and strategies

- Learn information and content from writing

Writing is much like teaching; you have to master your subject area in order to share it in an effective manner. When children write to inform an audience, for example, they are learning more about their subject area, and the sheer fact that they are writing develops awareness of genre and writing ability. Oh, you may groan. "I don't know how to teach writing!" or "My kids can't even create an effective paragraph!" or "They can only write a paragraph, so I don't expect more."

These are all valid points, but they don't teach kids how to write effectively or show them how to write in a content area. If your students don't know *how* to tackle writing, it is time to directly teach what they don't know so that they can be successful. Children can write at multiple times in the content workshop:

- During reading, to help construct meaning and comprehend

- After reading, to learn facts and vocabulary and to develop conceptual understanding

- In response to research to produce a report, expository piece, or other writing piece

Reading Journals and Information Logs

When students are reading, they will also be writing about their reading. The workshop includes time to read and time to write. During reading, the most important activity is for students to *read*, so you need to be very careful about how much you expect them to write in response to their reading. It is important to think of the purpose for writing during reading.

Students will write while reading in order to log information and to take notes that will be used for class discussion and writing assignments. They will write to note tidbits of information they find important and to record new and interesting vocabulary. Equally important, they should *not* be asked to write in order to prove to you that they read. Rather than having students write in response to reading as a way to prove that they were productive, trust them enough and engage them in books enough that their desire to read interesting information will be spontaneous.

Writing to Learn

Writing instruction needs to be embedded in the regular school day expectations, and it needs to occur during a separate writing workshop mini-lesson. These two types of writing instruction might look a bit different, but both provide explicit instruction for students as a learning on-ramp.

Another type of writing instruction occurs when children write nonfiction pieces. Because children learn by writing, they need to learn how to write so that the writing becomes a vehicle for learning rather than an impediment. Remember, we teach explicitly through the mini-lesson. Your mini-lesson is the centerpiece of the workshop and gives you the opportunity to provide many learning on-ramp opportunities for students. Your mini-lesson scaffolds student learning and becomes an on-ramp to learning *if* you do the following:

- Have a clear objective
- Use visuals and organizational tools
- Make your thinking transparent and tell what, how, and why
- Demonstrate

Scaffolding Writing Instruction

When we teach writing, we give students an on-ramp to learning. The writing on-ramp to learning shows students explicitly how to write and respond in ways that meet your expectations. Don't assign students writing without first modeling, explaining your thinking, and guiding them through the "how-to." Then leave them free to explore their reading, thinking, and the information they come across as they read with purpose and intent.

Embedded Writing Instruction

Every time you expect children to know how to do something, you need to tell them what you want in a nurturing and supportive way. I don't know how many times I have seen the look of "why didn't you just say so" on the face of a student I was working with in writing. We *think* they should see what we see or understand what we are expecting. But often, we are not clear. So, embedded writing instruction occurs when you are expecting students to write something in response to reading as a thinking tool or an organizational tool. Rather than requiring a full mini-lesson during writing workshop, embedded instruction occurs during the reading and content instruction. I might embed instruction when demonstrating how to do these tasks:

- Use a sticky note pad for note-taking

- Use a graphic organizer or other information-recording sheet to record new facts and information

- Use a notebook to record observations

- Use an organizer to memorialize steps in a process

- Write an informal summary

When embedding writing instruction, follow a few simple steps. You want to do whatever it takes to make sure students own the process you are asking them to use so that they can work independently and focus on their reading. Remember, giving them time to read and to fall under the spell of reading provides them the opportunity to learn and process information.

To embed writing instruction, focus on visualizing what you want the final product to look like, describing that in clear words, modeling it, and displaying the model somewhere in the classroom so students can easily access it when they need a reminder.

If I wanted to teach students how to take a jot on a sticky note, I would be clear in my expectations, so the age-old student-teacher guessing game wouldn't occur, which goes something like this:

> *Students, I want you to take notes today when you are reading. It is important to note information while you are reading. Use the sticky pads in the group baskets so you can mark the page and take the note at the same time. Later, I will check your books to see how many sticky notes you wrote.*

*Student: Okay, she wants me to write some notes on here when I read.
I might as well get that over with first so I don't forget. I wonder
how many I should do. Oh, hey, Jack over there has three out.
I'll do three too. Hmmm . . . man . . . this is hard. I wonder
what I should take the note on. I'll just do all three on the first
paragraph, then it will be done.*

Sound familiar? I know how this goes so well from so many years of not being clear and not modeling and then feeling exasperated that my students didn't get it. Well, they didn't get it because I didn't give them the opportunity to do so: I didn't show them how. Clear, embedded instruction would look more like this:

*Today we are going to take notes while we are reading. (I give a
purpose.) I want you to take notes because when you stop and
think about what you read, it helps you to comprehend the text
and organize information in your heads. You are going to take
between three to five notes on the sticky pad today. (I give a
clear goal.) When you take the note, please use handwriting that
you or I can reread. Lately, we have been getting sloppy and I
cannot read your writing, and admit it—some of you can't read
your own writing. That doesn't do us any good because you are
going to review these notes later. (I give more explanation to
make the task clear.) When you take a note, I want it to look
something like this. On this chart, the big square is a sticky
note—you have to pretend to see it. You will take a note by
stopping your reading at a point where you think you have read
something important. Think about that idea and put it in a few
words. Watch me. (I demonstrate.) Okay, so today when you
write your sticky notes, stop while reading, think of what was
important, and write it down in just a few words. THEN,
place the sticky note on the page in the book where you read
the information. Put the sticky note at the edge like a flag.
(I demonstrate.)*

When focusing on embedded writing instruction, it is best to tell students these key expectations:

- What you want them to do

- Why you want them to do it

- How they should do it

The Content-Rich Reading & Writing Workshop

> **Ways to Embed Writing Within Other Lessons**
>
> Have students:
>
> - Take notes on a sticky note pad
> - Record information on a graphic organizer or other information-recording sheet
> - Record observations
> - Record steps in a process
> - Write a quick-write to record their thinking
> - Write a summary

Combining Expectation With Effective Assignments

All of your students can be successful writing any of these assignments as long as they know how to begin and have support to keep them going. Give them models for constructing and sequencing writing. Children need direct instruction and scaffolds that give them the organization and guidelines they need to be successful when writing (National Writing Project & Nagin, 2006).

Content-Based Writing Workshop

When you focus the content workshop time on writing, it is often at the point within a unit of study when you are showing children how to complete their integrated project or writing assignment. This is when you shift from helping children read, learn facts, and improve their comprehension and study skills to learning how to write. Refer to Chapter 8 for a full description of planning processes.

Much like the reading instruction focus described in Chapter 2, the writing workshop begins with a mini-lesson, provides children time to write in class, and then closes with a wrap-up or share, (See Figure 4.1 on page 72.) During the mini-lesson you slow your teaching down and make the *how* of writing transparent. See pages 108–110 for workshop details.

Mini-Lesson

To make your mini-lesson effective, you need to show your students exactly what you expect, modeling the writing and discussing your thoughts out loud so they can see, hear, and watch you construct writing. You would discuss how you approach each assignment depending on what the assignment expects children to do.

Workshop

During the workshop, you circulate, meeting with individuals and groups, providing exact, on-the-spot feedback. The focus is to help children write *while* they are writing. This is a shift

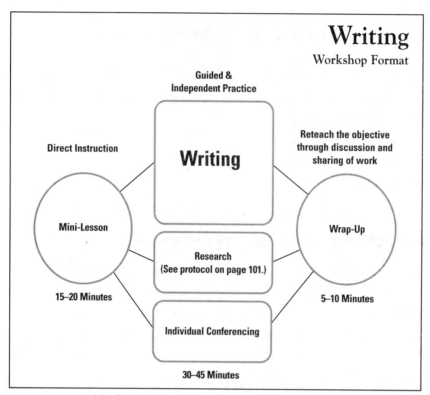

Figure 4.1: Writing workshop format

from having children write at home and then critiquing their work. During the workshop, you help them think about their work, refer to the modeling and expectations you laid out in the lesson, and then coach and encourage them as needed.

Focus

You are showing, and children are doing. You are definitely not red-marking papers to judge and evaluate; instead, you are giving clear and supportive feedback.

Expecting less writing doesn't help students who don't know how to write to write. Rather, plan your lessons backward as described in Chapter 8. Begin with the project and your precise expectations for what students will do during the project; then outline the lessons you will need to teach so they know and understand how to complete the writing for the project.

Avoid the Expectation Slide

In addition to mentoring writers into adulthood, we need to expect enough of them that writing is motivating. I often hear middle and high school teachers speak with longing for students who can write one great paragraph. To ensure that students can write one great paragraph, less and less writing is expected until the expectations are so low that the assignments become mundane and unengaging. This is how the expectation slide occurs. If you find this is beginning to happen in your class, you can turn to your state standards for guidance. For example, the California sixth-grade standards for writing state: "Students write clear, coherent, and focused essays. The writing exhibits students' awareness of the audience and purpose. Essays contain formal introductions, supporting evidence and conclusions." In addition, under the subtitle *organization and focus* this standard is listed: "Create multiple-paragraph expository compositions." While these snippets don't give a clear picture of all California state standards, they do clearly state that students are to write longer pieces and to write well. When I find I am caught in a cycle of lowering my expectations (the downward slide), I boost myself by checking standards and calibrating my expectations with the recommendations. Once, when I felt exasperated with a group of sixth-grade students and had to remind myself of their grade-level standards, the biggest eye-opener I had was that writing only a paragraph was a third-grade standard.

Expect your students to write often and to write a lot. Expect assignments to get the job done rather than to be a specific length. But beware—not expecting enough writing from upper-grade students conveys the implicit message that they are not capable of more.

Upper-grade students should be writing multiparagraph assignments, and they need to be shown how to do this. You may think it is easier to just teach them how to write one effective paragraph. But remember that during the process of writing, children reflect, analyze, and synthesize information and ideas and then pull them together in their own voice. This is extremely difficult to do in only a paragraph.

An Effective Content-Driven Writing Project

Cary Stolpestad, a fourth-grade teacher in Fresno, California, has developed an integrated social studies, reading, and writing unit around the California gold rush, a period that transformed the economy of the state, changed towns, and engendered economic conflicts among diverse groups. Cary's focus in the unit is to take an important period in history, plan around the social studies standards, and ensure that children can analyze events and information and synthesize their own understanding of this historical time and its importance.

Cary's unit is a perfect example of the planning processes shared in Chapters 7 and 8, combined with effective writing instruction. Cary teaches the content by having the children focus their integrated projects on a demographic group they select themselves. They complete research, analysis, and writing focused on the group they've chosen and how the group was affected by the discovery of gold in California in 1848 and the subsequent gold rush of 1849 through 1860. The project has three parts: choosing a demographic group, conducting research and writing about the group and the gold rush, and creating a History Board to display their published writing and research. Cary gives each student a carefully designed project outline so that the children know exactly what is expected of them and how to do it. (See Figure 4.2.)

When thinking about designing a project outline for your class, remember to use the backward-planning tools in Chapter 8. Once you know exactly what you are going to teach, and what you expect of children, it is easy to compile a focus sheet for the unit of study.

Project Outline

Part 1: Selection of Demographic Group

After selection of your demographic group, you will be costumed as a person of that demographic group during the gold rush era, and you will have a sepia-tone photograph taken of you. Begin thinking about whom you have become. As you research the gold rush, and your demographic group, continue to ponder how your fictitious persona feels about living through this historical event.

Part 2: Research, Analysis, and Writing

You will research your demographic group and how the group was affected before, during, and after the discovery of gold in California on January 24, 1848, and the subsequent gold rush of 1849–1860. Research materials will include:

1. California Vistas, Our Golden State social studies text book
2. Manchester GATE Internet research site
   http://www.fresno.k12.ca.us/schools/s031/resources/caproject/caproject06l inks.htm
3. Library research texts and trade books
4. Primary sources and biographies
5. Historic maps and sea routes
6. "The Gold Rush" PBS video
7. Teacher supplied handouts and supplemental information

Using the researched and analyzed information, you will write/create the following (all will be done in class):

1. "Summary of the Gold Rush" research paper
2. "How the California Gold Rush Affected (demographic group)" research and opinion paper
3. "(demographic group's) Population During the Gold Rush" Excel line plot
4. "1850 Population of California" Excel demographic circle chart
5. Bibliography of research material using easybib.com

Part 3 : Persona Development

You will develop your gold rush fictitious persona taking historical care to be accurate in his/her skills, abilities, and attributes. You will develop and write (all will be done in class):

1. "Autobiography of (persona's name)"
2. "(persona's name) Journal" – a one-year personal journal that must contain:
   a. 10 one-page accurately dated entries handwritten in the present tense recording events such as
      i. hearing the news of gold's discovery
      ii. traveling from home to the mother lode

Figure 4.2: Gold rush project outline

iii. life in the gold camps, boom towns, and gold
rush-related geographical areas

iv. deciding to go home/deciding to remain in
California

v. traveling home/making California home

b. personal emotions to everyday life and historical events

c. plentiful and accurate use of gold rush vocabulary

Part 4: Assemble Gold Rush History Board

You will be given the opportunity to publish all written work and compile it with
your Excel data charts, sepia-tone persona's photograph, and all other
supplemental research pictures onto your history board. This is the final part of
the project and will be done at home. The specific directions for placement of
your materials are on the next page.

Figure 4.2: Gold rush project outline continued

Student Writing Assignment

In Cary's first writing assignment for the project, students research their demographic group
and also research the gold rush era. The children then compose an expository essay. Cary has
the children do all of the writing during her writing workshop. She holds mini-lessons on how
to write the essay, focusing on the outline of the paper. By teaching the outline of the essay,
Cary helps children understand what they need to do and gain experience with the expository
text structure. See Figure 4.3 on page 76 for an example of Cary's teaching steps to help
children learn how to take notes and write an expository essay. She has students take notes on
note cards and in a notebook. Figures 4.4–4.6 on pages 77–78 show an example summary and
photos of student history boards.

On-Ramp to Learning ▶ **Writing On-Ramp**

Students need "on-ramps" to help them accelerate their learning in order to:

◆ be engaged

◆ practice writing more and often

◆ enjoy and find fulfillment in writing rather than anxiety and tears

– Help students learn to write by scaffolding writing so they can
be successful. *Tell, show, tell.*

– Make each step explicit so students can see what to do,
and how to think and reflect upon their writing.

Writing
"Summary of the Gold Rush"

After much research, analysis, and discussion, have the students orally sequence the events of California's gold rush. Model how to take notes of the sequencing and how to group into three major paragraphs. Students are responsible for reproducing their own copy of the notes as they will use them to produce their own "Summary of the Gold Rush." The following is a teacher's sequencing plan to use as needed to prompt students:

First Paragraph:
- January 24, 1848, James Marshall found gold in the American River near Coloma.
- Marshall was building a sawmill for Captain John Sutter.
- Sutter and Marshall did experiments to determine if it truly was gold.
- Sworn to secrecy
- May 12, 1848, Sam Brannan spread the news about gold through the streets of San Francisco.
- "Gold Fever" began to spread through California and then throughout the world.

Second Paragraph:
- Men from CA left jobs, ranchos, and families to go to gold field in 1848.
- By 1849, word of CA's gold rush reaches Mexico, South America, rest of United States, Europe, China, and Australia.
- Gold fever spreads through the world, and men called Forty-niners flocked to CA.
- Forty-niners traveled to CA by the sea route, Panama shortcut, or the overland route. The Chinese and Australians took a sea route across the Pacific Ocean.
- All miners arriving in 1849 discovered the easy gold was gone in 1848.
- Food and supplies were scarce in the gold fields, so prices were sky high.

Third Paragraph:
- The people that succeeded during the gold rush were the ones that either:
    — arrived in 1848 to get the easy gold.
    — sold food, supplies, or services to the miners.
    — were the very few that were lucky enough to strike it rich.
- Frustrated, many poor, unlucky miners left California and returned home penniless.
- Some miners were too broke to pay for the trip home, so they remained in California and worked for large mining corporations as poorly paid workers.
- Other broke miners left the mother lode and settled in another part of California where they began farms or other businesses.
- A few miners who struck it rich headed for home, or remained in California to spend their gold to start a new life in a new land.

Figure 4.3: Essay Explanation Sheet

Summary of California's Gold Rush

On January 24, 1849, James Marshall found a couple of pea sized nuggets in the American River near Coloma. He was building a saw mill for John Sutter. Unsure if they were real gold, Marshall took the nuggets to Elizebeth Wimmer, who tossed them into a pot of lye. The nuggets survived the lye. Then Marshall hit a nugget with a rock. The nugget flattened. Last, Marshall and John Sutter did some weight tests from an old encyclopedia and determined that it really was gold. Sutter and Marshall swore to keep the discovery of gold a secret, yet they didn't, and couldn't keep Sam Brannan quiet. On May 12, 1848, Brannan ran through San Francisco yelling about the discovery of gold in the south fork of the American River. Brannan did this after he had bought up all of the mining supplies and had them ready to sell at his store for a high price.

In 1848, Californios and Americans living in California went to the Mother Lode and quickly got the easy placer gold. They left everything behind: ranchos, jobs, and families, when they went to the diggings. By 1849, the world got wind of gold in California. Men from Mexico, Chile, the United States of America, China, Europe, and Australia rushed to California. The gold seekers rushed to California because of "gold fever". Forty-Niners could get to California sailing around The Horn, sailing and walking across the Isthmus of Panama, or going overland. The Chinese crossed the Pacific Ocean in junks and Australians also crossed the Pacific Ocean in clipper ships. When the Forty-Niners arrived in California, they found more high prices than they did gold. The gold was scarce because the Californios had the easy gold in their pokes.

Some successful folk in the Gold Rush were people who lived in California in 1848, business owners who sold supplies or did services for miners and a lucky few who struck it rich. Angry because the gold was scarce, some miners gave up and went home and others stayed in California to start a new life. Some were too poor to go home and joined mining companies. The lucky few who struck it rich either went home or stayed in California. The discovery of gold was an important part of California.

Figure 4.4: Sample of student writing from Cary's fourth-grade class

Figures 4.5–4.6: Student project boards showing all components of Cary's unit

PART II

Making It Work in Your Classroom

It is feast or famine in our classrooms. We are either over-relying on teaching reading strategies during our literacy block *or* we aren't teaching any reading strategies at all during our literacy block (Block et al., 2002; Duffy, 2002; Hirsch, 2003; National Institute of Child Health and Human Development [NICHHD], 2000; Vacca, 2002). If you have been in a workshop setting for many years, you might recognize that glazed look upper graders adopt when assigned another text-to-self connection assignment. Or, if you haven't taught in a workshop for long (or ever), you may wish to leave your work-sheet packets and long textbooks assignments far behind you, as *doing* the work sheet is often as difficult for kids to figure out as *the content* they are supposed to learn through the exercise.

Of course, we want our students to connect to learning, but to assume that all kids will grow into lovers of reading and knowledge through a steady diet of text connections or textbook assignments is off base. This just doesn't nurture long-term learning. When was the last time you talked about *how* you made a connection to a book? Usually, I talk about the book, the content of the book, and what it meant to me. I do not describe *how* I made the text connection to my best friend. Rather, I describe my thinking and feelings, or the connection itself. Today's seventh and eighth graders will be poised to take national tests like the SAT for entrance into college in just four years. Have they even begun to analyze text for the author's viewpoint or use of literary devices? If not, it is time to step away from over-nurturing readers' metacognition and focus on teaching them to apply their metacognitive strategies to the process of learning important information (Jetton & Alexander, 2004; Pressley, 2002a; Vacca, 2002).

In short, focus on the effective implementation of rigorous content work designed to foster interest and motivation in students. Students should know and understand reading and writing strategies and *use* the strategies to read and write rigorous work of value in connected classrooms (Brown, 2002; Duffy, 2002; Shanahan, 2004; Stahl, 2006; Stahl & Fairbanks, 2006). This section will show you how to make rich content teaching work in your classroom.

CHAPTER 5

Foster a Learning Apprenticeship
The Benefits of a Connected Classroom

"Teach reading comprehension strategies" may be a tired mantra, but in recent years comprehension strategies have garnered our attention for a real reason. Children who are not proficient readers in the upper grades often don't comprehend texts well, and research shows that the children lack skill in using reading strategies (Chall, 2000; Pearson & Raphael, 2003; Pressley, 2000, 2002a, 2002b). Numerous studies point to a basic set of reading strategies that should be taught and mastered. Differences exist, however, in what research suggests works in improving student reading abilities. For example, a few studies indicate that some comprehension strategies are learned effectively through practice and do not need to be explicitly taught. Other studies refute this point and call for direct, explicit instruction of all strategies.

So what does this mean for our classrooms? When trying to decide what is best based on the research, I look at the information available in front of me that I gather from the most important resource—the children. As you plan instruction, consider the following:

- The socioeconomic makeup of the class

- The number of English learners

- The most recent state test scores or district assessment scores

- The most recent classroom-based reading assessment

- The notes from classroom observations of children reading and writing

What do these indicators show? If any of them show you that a child may be facing a barrier to learning to read, then don't hesitate to be explicit and direct in your instruction of all strategies (Duffy, 2002). Give children time to practice and move at the speed of learning.

The Speed of Learning

The speed of learning isn't so fast-paced as to leave the children behind in the dust of textbooks flying, but it certainly shouldn't drag either. We have no time to waste when educating our children. Instruction needs to target what they need to know, move at a pace that is motivating and engaging, and support all learners so they have the chance to understand (Perry, Turner, & Meyer, 2006). Overall, the speed of learning is based on a no-nonsense classroom philosophy that we share with the children from day one:

- You belong here.

- You are part of the community.

- As a group we won't accept behavior that gets our learning off-track.

- We are moving forward.

- I will support you.

- You will understand.

Explanation Meets Apprenticeship

For years I harbored romantic notions about how the children in my class would learn. I truly thought that the thematic units I rolled out—which included cooking, drawing, cutting and pasting, coloring, and completing cleverly decorated math sheets (in the theme, of course!)— would entice learners to spontaneously become engaged in learning, and knowledge would spring forth from my efforts. While this may have worked for some children, unfortunately, I know it didn't work for most.

I have always taught in classrooms filled with children learning English, children from homes with few reading materials, and children who faced numerous challenges to make it to school every day. These children needed me to teach them information and strategies in a way that they could readily learn, preparing them for the next grade and future schooling. They really didn't need a theme-based curriculum; what they needed was a curriculum filled with content and strategies that naturally connected ideas and information in a way that was motivating and engaging and focused on developing their knowledge base.

My aim was to start children on an apprenticeship in learning, but along the way I didn't focus on standards and grade-level expectations; instead, I focused on themes. I was avoiding a direct-explanation method, which seemed to narrow the curriculum and ensure an only-one-right-answer stance in the classroom. I thought I was choosing a thinking, meaning-centered curriculum, but I wasn't. Today's classroom needs to focus on both direct explanation and apprenticeship (Stahl, 2006). Direct explanation is explicit teaching. A classroom that combines reveling in content with explicit teaching ensures learning. A workshop is just the format to bring these two methods together because in a workshop children can learn through extended conversations in which thinking and learning about text are the focus (Klinger & Vaughn, 2004).

How a Workshop Format Apprentices Learners and Thinkers

A workshop format includes a mini-lesson, independent practice using a variety of texts, and a reflective wrap-up. Rather than focusing on students getting the one exact answer (content regurgitation), the workshop structure helps students learn many facts through the application of reading and writing strategies (cognitive apprenticeship) (Stahl, 2006). (See Figure 5.1.)

Apprentice thinking and learning through the following means:

- Organizing instruction into 20-minute segments

- Delivering instruction in a direct, explicit manner, focusing on telling, modeling, and then telling

- Providing immediate opportunity to practice the discussed strategy in context

- Reflecting with the group on what worked, who learned what, and why

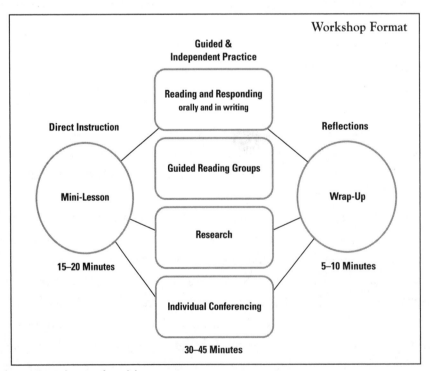

Figure 5.1: Architecture of a workshop

Explicit Teaching Works

Yes, explicit teaching works when the focus is children. The goal of explicit teaching should be to guide student thinking from a point of not knowing to a point of understanding (Duffy, 2002; Simpson & Nist, 2002). Effective explicit teaching doesn't focus only on transmitting knowledge to be regurgitated later on a test. Most important, it should be rigorous.

All students do have the intellectual ability to participate in rigorous work. It does have to be scaffolded to their level and designed to meet appropriate grade-level standards (Allington, 2001). That said, all students may not be open to learning, or they may not know how to support themselves in the activity. That is precisely why a reading and writing workshop, or a participatory literacy block, is essential. Reading and writing workshops naturally encourage students to interact with information and texts and to *do* something with the information and facts they gather. Merely gathering information and reusing it on a test isn't sufficient. Classrooms that focus only on transmitting information don't foster the intrinsic motivation needed by older students to succeed in school. The connected classroom does; it gets kids:

- Thinking and moving with a variety of texts
- Benefiting from carefully planned instruction
- Achieving, even when they aren't intrinsically motivated to do so

Defining the Connected Classroom

Connected classrooms support children. It is true that not all children who enter our classrooms want to be there. We have to make them want to be there and encourage them every step of the way. You may believe this is out of your control. But it isn't. Our locus of control extends from the start of our school day to the time when the children leave. At my school that is roughly between 8 a.m. and 3 p.m. We control everything that occurs during those hours. The essential ideas of connected classrooms keep us focused on the kids, and help us keep our focus on our locus of control. (See Figure 5.2.)

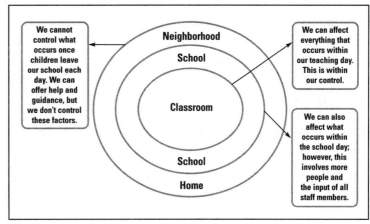

Figure 5.2: Locus of control diagram

Essential Ideas of Connected Classrooms

1. Teachers harness every moment to immerse children in information and opportunities to learn.

2. There is no "out." Children who act indifferent or give up easily are supported. Teachers may brainstorm collaboratively how to reach a child, because not reaching the child isn't an option.

3. Learning is scaffolded. Children aren't expected to know the information before they come to class. Children involved in classrooms that make learning "doable" give up less often than kids who don't receive support. Lessons are short and followed by a guided practice in the workshop (real reading and writing). Then each lesson is layered with another lesson, guided practice, and so on. This practice creates an underlying support structure for all students (Akhavan, 2006).

4. The work is fun and interesting. Content is cool and intriguing. People are hooked on nonfiction because they are curious about the world and how people live in it. We have to hook kids into loving the way the world works (science) and its past (history) as well.

5. Children are exposed to a large quantity of literature, nonfiction, and literary nonfiction.

6. The classroom atmosphere tells kids "you can" rather than "you can't." This begins with instruction and ends with a no-nonsense attitude. "It is important; it is your future" is a good message to begin with.

7. A sense of urgency fills the classroom. There is much for children to learn and limited time in our locus of control to complete the work. It is possible to close the achievement gap with purposeful content-rich workshop instruction. On the flip side, that means there is little room for complacency.

Strategies as Metacognitive Stepping-Stones

Research clearly points out that strategy instruction has been woefully under-taught (Pressley, 2002a, 2000b; Block et al., 2002; Pressley, Wharton-McDonald, Raphael, Bogner, & Roehrig, 2002; Pearson & Raphael, 2003). There's an achievement slump that occurs on test scores once children leave the comfort of the primary grades, a phenomenon Chall and Jacobs have called "the fourth grade plunge" (2003). This slump doesn't just appear in test scores. Fourth graders often get behind in reading once the focus shifts from learning to read to content-based reading, and they often don't catch up (Snall 2004). On the other hand, the fact that strategies are under-taught doesn't indicate that we should put aside application. After students get a handle on one strategy, or three or four for that matter, they need to apply the strategy to content at their grade level. A fourth grader in California who learns to effectively use the strategy *Determine important information in text* should be using it to read about the California gold rush. Students need to be explicitly taught how to use reading comprehension strategies in content study.

I am not suggesting that children shouldn't read for pleasure and I am not saying that content reading is the be-all and end-all to our reading lives. I am suggesting, however, that content reading should be a large portion of what children do at school. If they don't have the opportunity to learn the content at school, they may have no other place to learn it. Students' knowledge base needs to develop rapidly. The more they know about the world, the more school and schoolwork appeal to them, the more important schoolwork becomes, and the easier reading and writing will become. Spending time reading content results in vocabulary growth, increased reading ability, proficiency in writing, and the development of content knowledge. As children learn about their world and talk and write about their ideas, their knowledge and confidence will develop. Knowledge is powerful; it gives children a future.

Knowledge Development

For years I assumed that the higher up I went on Bloom's taxonomy, the better my instruction was. The higher levels seemed more worthy, more glamorous, more ideal than the lower levels, especially the level of knowledge. This just isn't the case. Knowledge is just as important as synthesis and analysis. Think of the taxonomy as a flat structure rather than a pyramid. (See Figure 5.3, page 86.) A student needs to be versed in all parts of the taxonomy (Krathwohl, 2002). Our workshops cannot become too focused on *doing* without learning important facts, and our literacy blocks cannot get too focused on facts without opportunities for students to synthesize and analyze ideas and information. Focusing mini-lessons on a combination of knowledge structures is key to using content to drive your strategy instruction.

In fact, our English learners, our unmotivated students, our poor children, and our struggling readers need us to focus on everything it takes to help them become well-educated and be prepared for high school. They need a broad knowledge base, and then they need to know how to gather and analyze information on their own. (Stahl, Jacobson, Davis, & Davis, 2006). This is what precise, well-thought-out units focus on in content-centered workshops. Well-designed units guide students to learn facts *and* do something with the information in order to transfer knowledge gained in one situation to another situation, and guide them to effectively communicate their ideas about complex material (Alvarez & Mehan, 2004).

A Revision of Bloom's Taxonomy (Krathwohl, 2002)

Cognitive Processes Dimension

	Remember	Understand	Apply	Analyze	Evaluate	Create
Factual Knowledge						
Conceptual Knowledge						
Procedural Knowledge						
Metacognitive Knowledge						

Knowledge Dimension

A Revision of Bloom's Taxonomy (Krathwohl, 2002)

Description of Knowledge Dimensions

	Description	Examples
Factual Knowledge	Basic information to be acquainted with in a discipline	Terminology Specific details
Conceptual Knowledge	The interrelationships among basic elements within a structure to enable them to function together	Classification and categories Principles and generalizations Theories and models
Procedural Knowledge	How to do something, methods and criteria for using skills, methods, techniques	Subject-specific skills and algorithms Subject-specific methods and techniques Knowledge of criteria for knowing when to use appropriate skills or methods
Metacognitive Knowledge	Knowledge of cognition and awareness of one's own cognition	Strategic knowledge Cognitive tasks Self-knowledge

Knowledge Dimension

Figure 5.3: A revision of Bloom's Taxonomy

Helping Students Acquire Knowledge

There are times when we need to practice synthesizing information and evaluating what and why something occurred. But without developing a large knowledge base, it is impossible to effectively interpret, analyze, and evaluate. In fact, we have multiple knowledge "compartments" in our brains. Schraw (2006) suggests in his research that we have three knowledge categories: declarative knowledge, procedural knowledge, and self-regulatory knowledge. (See Figure 5.4.) Schraw's classification of knowledge helps us think about what kinds of knowledge children are developing in our classrooms. They aren't all the same.

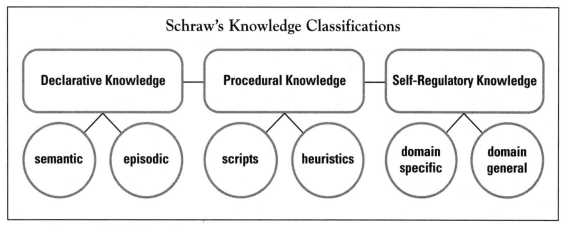

Figure 5.4: Schraw's Knowledge Classifications diagram

Declarative Knowledge

Declarative knowledge is a broad category. It includes all knowledge we develop regarding facts, concepts, and the relationships among concepts that create an integrated understanding of them (Schraw, 2006). Declarative knowledge also includes the schema we develop to understand abstract concepts. A schema is a structure in our brains that helps us organize large amounts of information into a conceptual understanding. Basically, schemas help us integrate information and form a mental model (Schraw, 2006; Senge et al., 2000).

Procedural Knowledge

Procedural knowledge is knowledge about how to do things, and it ranges from simple to complex. Procedural knowledge includes scripts, algorithms, and heuristics. Scripts help our brain organize how to complete an activity like brushing our teeth or driving a car. They help us carry out day-to-day activities without having to pay attention to our thinking (Schraw, 2006).

Algorithms, or rules for solving a problem, are useful when we want to solve a well-defined problem. You teach children algorithms when you show them how to solve a math problem using specific steps.

Heuristics are what we use to solve problems. A heuristic is like a rule of thumb (Schraw, 2006). As teachers we use heuristics to plan differentiated instruction after reviewing student assessment. We aren't sure what exactly will work to help the child read better, but we have a set of paths, or skills, to follow that generally help, and we use them to change direction during a lesson.

Self-Regulatory Knowledge

Schraw defines this category as "the knowledge of how to regulate our memory, thought, and learning" (2006, p. 250). This is the knowledge we have about ourselves, the way we learn, and the skills we possess (or lack) in order to learn. This category is divided into two sections: domain-specific knowledge and domain-general knowledge (Schraw, 2006).

Domain-specific knowledge is what we know about specific conceptual areas and topics, including specific words and concepts associated with content areas (Akhavan, 2007). For example, I have broad domain knowledge in the areas of education and instruction, but a rather small body of knowledge regarding computer science.

Domain-general knowledge is metacognitive knowledge. It includes strategy knowledge and regulatory skills such as planning, monitoring, and evaluating our learning (Schraw, 2006). In the content-rich literacy block, you teach children domain-specific knowledge when you teach information from the specific subject area, such as science or social studies. You teach domain-general knowledge when you teach children a learning strategy.

When students become good at school, and good at learning, they have a wide variety of learning strategies to pull from their metacognitive toolkit. However, research suggests that successful learners actually rely on a small set of general strategies that they adapt for different tasks (Schraw, 2006). These strategies include the following (Brown, 2002; Duffy, 2002; Schraw, 2006; Tovani, 2000):

- Identifying main ideas
- Making inferences
- Determining importance in text
- Summarizing
- Visualizing
- Creating graphic organizers

Skills Instruction Versus Strategy Instruction

If we are working on developing student ability to use strategies while learning content, we need to carefully guide our mini-lessons. You might wonder, When is the activity we are teaching a skill and when is it a strategy? Schraw's knowledge classification makes it easier to think about this idea. When we consciously apply a strategy to learn, we are using domain-general, or metacognitive knowledge, and that is learning and using a *strategy* (Schraw, 2006). When we automatically follow a path or heuristic to solve a problem while reading, we are applying a *skill*. While we may become skilled at using graphic organizers, the act of choosing a graphic organizer is a reading comprehension strategy. When we automatically chunk words in order to pronounce them, we are applying a reading skill. Yes, our students need both skills and strategies, and yes, we need to teach comprehension skills as well as word-attack skills. But keep your eye on the ball—if we have upper-grade students who can't *think* about their reading once they have decoded it, they are on the fast track to becoming disengaged from reading, school, and knowledge development. Providing academic scaffolds within powerful content-focused mini-lessons helps you and your students negotiate the complex balance of learning, motivation, and grade-level standards (Alvermann, Fitzgerald, & Simpson, 2006; Underwood & Pearson, 2004).

On-Ramp to Learning ▸ **Apprentice Learning!**

◆ First, provide students with direct teaching. Think: *What do I want students to learn?* Show them, tell them, model for them.

◆ Second, focus on students as apprentices to the knowledge you are teaching. Ask:

How do I slow down so they can learn the material/strategy?

How do I guide and coach them so they can become experts?

How do I give feedback and reteach when they don't get it right the first time (or the second, or third, or ...)?

CHAPTER 6

Harness the Power of Content

How Teaching Protocols Help You and Your Students

Harnessing the power of content means balancing your teaching between lessons designed to show students how to do something (such as comprehend what they are reading) and those that develop knowledge (by gathering facts and synthesizing information into new understandings) (Long, Wilson, Hurley, & Pratt, 2006; Mayer & Wittrock, 2006.) As I mentioned earlier, it is time to stop thinking about content teaching and learning as separate from reading and writing workshops and start thinking about content teaching as a balance between reading comprehension abilities and fact-learning/information-processing strategies.

Teaching Comprehension Strategies

"Now, what a minute," you might be thinking. "I thought we were supposed to steer *away* from focusing on comprehension strategies." It is true that I made a case for focusing on content, but we still need to teach comprehension strategies. Your students who struggle to read content (the textbook, for example) won't spontaneously know how to do that if you simply assign a lot of content reading (Brown, 2002; Dreher, 2002). Children often fail to apply their knowledge of reading strategies to their reading, and they often fail to apply their knowledge of how to locate information in nonfiction texts (Dreher, 2002). They may know how to apply strategies with us by their side, but they don't do it when they are reading alone. We also need to teach comprehension strategies to good readers who are learning to navigate new types of texts and different types of reading. Even college students often need help with approaching and reading a variety of difficult textbooks (Simpson & Nist, 2002).

Comprehension is undertaught; by that I mean that it doesn't go deep. Our instruction needs to focus on developing children who use strategies consciously and spontaneously so that they have the potential to become expert readers. Expert readers use reading comprehension strategies *without prompting from others* (Neufeld, 2005). Expert readers are self-regulated. Comprehension strategies are also undertaught because most instruction occurs with fiction and other narrative texts. Our students in upper grades getting their first big dose of content reading need help, and we are going to have to show them how to learn. They need to learn *how* to apply the strategies in all the reading they encounter, and they need to become self-regulated. Struggling readers need us to help them improve their reading abilities, including fluency, vocabulary, and word work skills (Nagy, Berninger, & Abbott, 2006). With other students we need to show them how to read nonfiction resources, understand them, and set a purpose for reading for information. Content instruction develops background knowledge, and knowing a lot of general information about the world and specific information about different topics improves comprehension (Jetton & Alexander, 2004). Content instruction also develops vocabulary, and children with highly developed vocabularies tend to be better readers.

We tend to think that once children know how to read, they stay at grade level. This often isn't the case as readers move up through the grades and encounter increasingly denser and more complex informational texts . Refer to Chapters 2 and 3 for a variety of ways to teach reading in the content-based workshop. A resource for structured vocabulary lessons that focus on developing student reading ability and aid comprehension in only a few minutes a day is *Accelerated Vocabulary Instruction* (Akhavan, 2006).

As we become skilled in teaching the content-based workshop, instruction will alternate between days spent teaching reading comprehension and teaching content learning strategies. (See Figure 6.1 for an example of this type of planning.)

Day 1	Day 2	Day 3	Day 4	Day 5
Teach first content lesson of the unit.	Continue content lesson of the unit—show streaming video from Web.	Show use of two-column note-taking strategy.	Practice using two-column note-taking strategy.	Introduce next important content concept of the unit.
Day 6	Day 7	Day 8	Day 9	Day 10
Continue next important content concept of the unit discussion and reinforce two-column note-taking— "get the gist."	Partner students to read textbook— teach "get the gist" strategy again.	Students read independently— work with small groups on summarizing.	Students read independently— work with small groups on summarizing.	Confer with students individually— check "get the gist" sheets. Double-check they understood concepts in textbook.

Figure 6.1: Balance between reading lessons and content lessons

Content Learning Strategies

Learning strategies help children remember information. Think of content-learning strategies as "study skills plus." Supporting children as they interact with content and learn facts and information means guiding them to take control of their learning. You will need to push them—just a little—to take ownership. They need to learn strategies to help them retain and recall information. Most students don't consciously use *any* strategy to help them learn information. I'll bet our own repertoires are also small.

Quickly jot down the study skills you remember using in high school or during your undergraduate work. What skills did you list? How long is your list? Mine is fairly short.

- Read assignment. (Yes, this is important to list: some students skip this part.)

- Highlight important information and key terms. (Most of the time my textbook would turn yellow because I highlighted everything.)

- Write notes from the highlighted passages. (This was laborious, as I highlighted indiscriminately.)

- Reread to study for the test. (I had to do this because my notes were long and the book was *over*-highlighted, so I had trouble picking out what might be on the test.)

If I were a student today, I would give myself a D in study skills. I think that I earned higher than an F because at least I did something, but my skills weren't streamlined or helpful. Overall, they were rather unsophisticated. I did not use graphic organizers, visually represent information, create vocabulary lists, use two-column note taking, summarize information, create webs of information, or even know how to take a jot note. Over the years, I've worked with many students who had no idea how to approach content research or studying. Students need a repertoire of content-learning strategies, or study skills plus. It isn't enough to expose them to these strategies—they have to own them. Children need to use the strategies with automaticity. Here's what focusing on content-learning strategies can do for children:

- Provide multiple opportunities to interact with information

- Provide thinking models

- Develop knowledge

- Expose them to a variety of subjects and information

- Help them *own* information

- Provide ways to remember and recall information

Goals of a Study Skills Plus Unit

A study skills plus unit has two goals: to teach content-learning strategies and to provide information. There will be days when you focus on teaching information, and there will be other days when you focus on teaching how to use a strategy to organize, remember, and recall information. Either way, all instruction should actively engage students; even when teaching information you will want to avoid transmission-style teaching where you lecture.

Active Instruction Supports Students

In transmission teaching, the teacher lectures, and students are expected to learn, remember, and recall information based on the lectures. Students are not involved in the lesson or the learning—in fact, they are usually sitting in their desks dutifully copying off the board or filling in packets of work sheets (Jetton & Alexander, 2004; Murphy & Mason, 2006).

Active and engaging instruction involves students in the transaction between thought and information (Baker & Brown, 2002; Guthrie & Wigfield, 2000). In the transactional classroom, teachers do provide direct explanation of strategies and information, but the focus is on the interaction between the children and the information (Williams, 2002). It isn't enough if student *hear* facts and information; they need to *interact* with information and *apply* strategies to figure out meaning on their own.

I know firsthand that focusing on transmission doesn't help children learn information. It only ensures that they *hear* it (well, maybe, and only if they are listening). When I was teaching a large group of children learning English about the Native Americans living in different California regions, I *thought* that what I needed to do was tell them everything there was to know about each tribe and the region they lived in. I read dutifully from the text, used visuals, and carefully went over vocabulary. I employed all of the teaching strategies I learned to make the content comprehensible (comprehensible information is a key idea in teaching English as a second language). I thought I had done such a great job teaching.

At the end of my three-week unit I found that while the students *seemed* engaged, *watching* me and *listening* to me, they retained little information. The end-of-unit test results were poor. At first, I assumed my test was inappropriately written, so I interviewed the children, allowing them to speak in Spanish if needed. Guess what I found out? My students had retained very little of the information. They didn't own it. They also didn't realize I had been showing them great content-learning strategies along the way. The problem: *I* was the one doing the *doing*. The students sat passively and listened, and when I was making a chart or writing down information, I didn't slow down my teaching and *show* the children my thinking or *explain* what I was doing and why. I fell into that classic teaching pitfall: I knew the information and thought if the children could just be exposed to it, they would be so engaged, they would learn. I forgot to involve them. I was stuck in a transmissive teaching stance. I wanted to give students information and I expected them to remember it for a test. I think of this as lecture and regurgitation. In short, it is transmissive teaching, and it just isn't as effective as transactional instruction.

To foster transactional instruction keep a focus on students as they attempt each of the following:

- Working with text and content

- Questioning ideas and information

- Forging their own viewpoints

- Understanding the viewpoints of scientists, historians, and authors

- Synthesizing information from multiple viewpoints

- Writing about their learning

- Using learning strategies purposefully and consciously

- Talking with one another and the teacher to develop understanding

Study Skills Plus Means Student Support

Transactional teaching alone is not enough. You need to buoy your students along by creating an atmosphere in which they know that they have time to learn information, and that you will support their efforts to understand how to use strategies. When kids think they can *get it right*, they will put forth more effort. You need to show your students how to do each of these tasks (Pressley, 2000):

- Apply a strategy

- Engage in purposeful practice

- Do something with the information they are gathering

- Be accountable for learning

Apply, Engage, Do, and Be

Think of the inflatable swimming floaters that parents blow up in summer and attach to their young children's arms before letting them swim for the first time. If our students are thrown into an assignment without clear explanations and abundant opportunities to learn *how*, they will sink. But if we give them floaters, showing them how and holding them responsible for doing so, they will swim. In essence, our students will respond and be successful. When you show your students how to apply a learning strategy while gathering information, they will have a better chance at learning the information and recalling it (Nokes & Dole, 2004). If they engage with peers and discuss their ideas and findings, they will have a real purpose for exploring information and studying. If you hold them accountable for learning, then they will know learning counts in the classroom.

Holding kids accountable is okay. Accountability isn't a gotcha—it helps students float along. If students are not held accountable, then they will learn that their reading, writing, and assignments don't matter to the teacher. There is really nothing worse than doing a lot of work when it doesn't matter to the teacher. So think of accountability in a positive light. Accountability means that you are providing engaging and purposeful reasons to learn information. It just isn't engaging for students to collect information to fill out a work sheet, or to sit quietly during third period and answer the end-of-chapter questions. It *is* engaging to learn information in order to discuss it with a peer group, or to complete a quick write, or to define new vocabulary words for the class. When you give students effective practice time after a transparent mini-lesson, hold them accountable for finishing the work assigned. They will learn, and your workshop will be productive for your students and you.

Apply, engage, do, and be means focusing on *answerability*. The Office online dictionary defines *answerability* as "responsibility for something, or an obligation to explain your actions to somebody." A study skills plus unit focuses on teaching a learning strategy so that students can apply it, engage with information, be active with the information, and use it in a meaningful way. Using the study skills plus lesson plan, you can ensure that you incorporate these four elements into several lessons in your unit. While the lesson plan is a great way to plan instruction, it also helps you stay on track when you're actually teaching.

Teaching Protocols Guide Content instruction

Keep on track by following a protocol for your workshop. *Following a protocol* might sound a bit formal, but this is what all good teachers do. They have a set pattern in their minds that they either consciously or unconsciously follow, which helps them maximize their instruction and engage students (El-Dinary, 2002). Our brains function on protocol knowledge. It is one type of knowledge we have about the world. We have unconscious protocols that help us with activities of daily living, such as brushing our teeth or driving to the market (Schraw, 2006; Sousa, 2006). Great teachers use protocols as well. They approach the time spent in the workshop in almost the same way each day. This helps them free up their thinking and teaching to focus on the children and their responses in order to modify for understanding and then move on (Afflerbach, 2000; Fisher, Schumaker, & Deshler, 2002).

Another dividend of following a protocol is that it enables you to keep an engaging pace. You want kids engaged with content and interested in your lesson. The proper pacing of your instruction is going to keep kids attentive to learning facts and information while actively engaging with content (Sinatra, Brown, & Reynolds, 2002). It is also going to give them opportunities to practice learning strategies while reading important content with you beside them as coach (Fisher, Schumaker, & Deshler, 2002).

Elements of an Effective Protocol

A protocol that works to teach content learning strategies includes these elements: (Brown, 2002; Duke & Pearson, 2002; Neufeld, 2005):

- Direct instruction
- Guided practice with small group-teaching
- Independent practice
- Wrap-up that reinforces the lesson objective

Direct Instruction

You begin the workshop by teaching something new to the children. This is your mini-lesson. Remember that this lesson is focused by the unit planning, discussed in Chapter 8. Your focus is to *directly teach* a learning strategy and make your teaching transparent so that the children can own the strategy after practice. (See Figure 6.2.)

Figure 6.2: Teaching area ready for direct instruction

Figure 6.3: Students working on information reports in a small group

Guided Practice With Small-Group Teaching

This is the actual workshop "work." The children focus on the content and apply the learning strategy you taught during the direct instruction to their own work. Depending upon the task, they may be researching, partner reading, conferring with each other, gathering information, writing summaries, using graphic organizers, or using the computer to gather information. (This is not an inclusive list of what children can do during a content-based workshop.)

And what are you doing? You may be conferring with students, helping them think their way through research and information, directing them to use a graphic organizer correctly, referring them to information that may be posted on the walls. You may also be leading small study groups. They provide a way to differentiate instruction. Some children need an extra shot of help, and this is the perfect time to reteach a strategy or go over information again. You can also meet with children who are ready to extend their learning. In that case you may show them a new learning strategy, discuss research pointers, or share a more difficult text. (See Figure 6.3.)

Independent Practice

While some children may have taken off right from the mini-lesson, not needing any help, others work with a peer or with you during the guided practice phase. Before the end of the workshop, it's important to ensure that all students work independently for a bit of time. This settles children into thinking and working habits. It helps them deeply internalize information you may ask them to present to their peers during the wrap-up or a subsequent lesson. You may want to use a signal partway through the workshop to let the students know that they are to work independently. Make sure they have a learning goal outlined so this time is productive and helpful instead of frustrating for children. (See Figure 6.4.)

Figure 6.4: Students working independently to complete project boards

Wrap-Up

My workshops used to come to an abrupt end. Usually, right before the bell rang, I would ask the children to quickly clean up. The children and I had run out of time! Now, I work to avoid that situation, as closure is important. During the wrap-up, children have time to organize new information and store it in their brains so that they can retrieve it the next day. Rushing over the end of a productive work time and rushing out of the class, or to the next "chunk" of the day, is unsettling. Wrap-up brings closure. I always reinforce the objective for the day by discussing the good work students were involved in. I jump-start the closure by sharing one or

Figure 6.5: The teacher recaps information at the end of the workshop.

two focused points and then let students discuss their thinking and learning. It is important to keep the wrap-up short and focused so it doesn't eat up the actual work time (which is the most important thing to have students do—engage!) (See Figure 6.5.)

Other Effective Protocols

The direct instruction, practice, wrap-up protocol is only one way to approach the block of time you have set aside to teach content in your workshop. Depending on the nature of the work and the learning goal for the day, you may choose to follow a different protocol to guide your work and the time your students spend in the workshop. There will be days you focus strictly on teaching information, days you teach learning strategies, and days when you help students become metacognitive about their learning (El-Dinary, 2002). Figures 6.6–6.8 provide three separate protocols you might use when focusing on teaching science or social studies in your workshop.

Fact Learning Protocol

Teach students to do the following steps:

1. Identify a section of a larger text. Survey text and visuals. Think about questions such as the following:

   What is the text structure?

   What information seems to be most important? (Look at bold words, section titles, and so on.)

   What key information is found in the graphs, photos, captions, and diagrams?

2. Read the section.

3. Think while reading. Do the following:
   - Stop.
   - Identify new information that seems to be the main idea of the text.
   - Jot a short statement about new information in your notebook.

4. Finish reading the section and then scan the text. Note any new information that now makes sense.

Make three passes over the text before moving on.

Survey, read, scan.

Figure 6.6: Fact Learning Protocol

Teach students to gather facts and information to complete reports and projects by focusing on surface-level and deep-processing strategies (Jetton & Alexander, 2004). Showing students how to copy relevant information from a text and recording reference information is surface-level processing. Directing students to think about the recorded facts and information is deep-level processing. Teach students to personalize or transform the information (Jetton & Alexander, 2004). Use the Research Organizer on page 149, Appendix S, when following this protocol. In your project outline, do the following:

1. State clearly the number of resources a student should explore for a given project.
2. Describe the expected number of sections, categories, or subgroups required for the project or report.
3. Provide at least one copy of the Research Organizer for each section, category, or subgroup required.

Research/Application Protocol

Teach students the following steps while completing research:

1. Identify the project focus and possible categories that I am researching. Record the title of the project and the category on the research sheet.
2. Locate 3–5 resources that provide information regarding the project and category.
3. Scan the text and determine if the resource is appropriate for the project. Ask the following questions:

    Is the resource credible?

    Does the resource provide facts, data, graphics, and/or relevant information?

    Is the source based on fact or opinion?

4. Record resource information and facts on the graphic organizer.
5. Stop and think about the information. Focus on what the information means in your own words. Ask the following questions:

    How does this information relate to my guiding questions?

    What do I think it means?

    Why do I think it is important?

    How does it relate to my topic focus or thesis?

    Record a few statements about your thinking in the column titled *Significance*.

Figure 6.7: Research/Application Protocol

Read/Think/Review Protocol

Focus students on when and where to apply comprehension strategies during reading of authentic texts and textbooks.

Teach students to follow these steps:

1. Identify a reading goal that matches the type of text to be read and students' learning needs.

2. Monitor comprehension by asking self-reflective questions, such as the following:

   Are there words I don't know?
   Are there sentences I don't understand?
   Are there sections that don't make sense?

3. Apply solutions to reading problems. Fix-up strategies include the following:
   Reread a word or phrase
   Skip a difficult word and revisit after reading a few sentences
   Chunk unknown words
   Look at word roots
   Look at diagrams and other print features for clues
   Make an informed guess
   Compare a word to similar words
   Compare a sentence/section to the sentence before and the sentence after
   Seek help from a peer

4. Reflect after reading. Think about questions such as the following:

   How well did I meet my reading goal?
   What section was difficult?
   What did I do to solve my reading problem?

Figure 6.8: Read/Think/Review Protocol

▶ **Study Skills Plus**

 ◆ Study skills are strategies that help students retain information.

 ◆ Provide thinking models to help students remember and recall.

 ◆ Help students own information by walking them through a step-by-step process to remember.

 ◆ Teach students how to comprehend, retain, and recall.

CHAPTER 7

Focus on Student Learning

Transparent Teaching Ensures Success for You and Your Students

C lear and focused teaching removes barriers and offers an opportunity for all students to learn facts and concepts in the content-rich workshop (Duke & Pearson, 2002). Clear and focused teaching is transparent, which means that children can clearly see what they are learning—and why. When learning a strategy, for example, a child understands the following:

■ How to practice the strategy

■ What the strategy looks like in practice

■ How to master the strategy

■ Why the strategy matters

Practices of Transparent Teaching

Communication and organization are at the heart of transparent teaching. Ironically, the more experienced we are as teachers, the easier it is for us to glide over processes that we internalized long ago—without providing the scaffolding that most learners need. By making the components of, and rationale for, any process or strategy explicit, we help students know what they're doing as well as why they're doing it. When we focus on our teaching being explicit, we are focusing on teaching directly. Teaching directly differs from "direct instruction." Instead of following a script of how to teach (a common practice in a direct instruction model), we are creating our own steps to follow, ensuring that *all* of our students understand what we are teaching and can *own* the learning.

Effective practices of transparent teaching include the following:

- Setting the scene

- Making connections

- Telling the *what*

- Telling the *how*

- Assessing

- Reteaching—or telling the students, "*We didn't get it so let's try again*"

Telling is an important concept in transparent teaching. Children shouldn't have to try to figure out what we want them to do or what we are trying to say (Brown, 2002). We need to buoy them along by just *telling* them what we want them to learn, try, do, or practice. The discovery comes from the construction of information as they do these things. No two children will perceive information in exactly the same way, and they can enhance each other's learning by sharing and discussing their thinking and learning as part of guided practice (Brophy, 2006; Sousa, 2006), So, *telling* isn't a negative idea; it is a positive way to help children know what they need to do so that they will be successful (Neufeld, 2005).

Setting the Scene

Setting the scene occurs before you begin teaching. When opening your content workshop for the day, pay attention to these three factors:

- Time—allot time for the workshop and stick to it. Routines are important and will save you a lot of angst. See Chapter 6 for more information on effective routines.

- Space—create a meeting space so that students can get up and move around to separate the workshop from the previous activity in your schedule. This gives children time to shake out their arms and legs. Upper graders do enjoy hanging out on the floor or at someone else's desk for class meeting time.

- Standards of behavior—from the first minute of the lesson set behavior standards. Let students know how you expect them to act while you are teaching. Be firm and consistent.

Making Connections

Establish connections between what kids are going to learn in class today and what they have learned previously. Ensure that information and language are comprehensible by making language concrete (Freeman & Freeman, 1998; 2003; Krashen, 2003). Use a chart, a book, or other item you can hold and display; create word cards; use sentence strips; or create key word cards or fact sheets. To make learning more than an aural experience, consider the following options:

- Create a visual—have chart paper and markers handy in order to write down what you are saying in a visual organizer. Charts are powerful mnemonic devices that remind students of learning and help them recall information (Sousa, 2006; Wolfe, 2001; Zull, 2002)

- Establish connections—connect new information to previously learned information (see Chapter 2 on prereading activities)

Telling the *What*

Be clear about the learning objective of the day. Prepare your students for what is going to happen in the mini-lesson, what they will do during the workshop, what things they should think about, attempt, or try. Don't think about the *what* as assignments they need to complete; the *what* is learning. What will they learn, what should they practice, and what will that look like while they are practicing it?

Telling the *How*

Children need to know *how* to do something for themselves. They can watch you do it, listen to you explain something, but they cannot practice until they know the steps to take (Graves, 2004; Neufeld, 2005; Neuman & Celano, 2006). You have to say how, over and over again, and in as many ways as possible until children know and understand. Be direct. You might say something like this:

- Watch me while I think through this text out loud. You are going to do what I do.

- You're going to read, and then put a sticky note on the page where you . . .

Phrases that are direct connect children to the *how*—they give the steps for them to try independently.

Assessing

Assessment is second in importance only to showing children and telling children how when teaching. You need to assess on multiple levels and in more than one way. Collect quantitative data that tell you in a numerical format what children know in relation to specific criteria.

There are multiple ways to collect this data, but in the content-based workshop it is helpful to collect data in ways that will inform your instruction. These include the following (Fountas & Pinnell, 2006; Snow, 2003):

- Giving a running record using a leveled text set

- Administering a paper-and-pencil test designed to assess a specific standard

- Using a rubric to assign a numerical result to student writing

You can also assess during instruction by checking for understanding. You can use quick whole-class management techniques such as these:

- Asking students to show thumbs-up as an answer to a question

- Having students write their answers on a small whiteboard and hold it up so you can see it

- Listening to student discussion during think/pair/share activities

- Conferring with individuals as they work

Reteaching

After assessing, reteach any strategy or point that the children didn't grasp. Before reteaching it is important to know exactly what the children didn't learn, so you can hone in on that particular point or information again. It is important to reteach only what is needed and only to those who need it (Lubliner, 2004). If the whole class didn't grasp a point, then reteach the whole group. If several students need help, then small groups are a better choice. Remember, the most important point during reteaching is to be *transparent* in your thinking, discussion, and directions—but in a different way than the first time. The children didn't learn it the first time through, so it is likely you need to modify your delivery. Techniques for reteaching include these:

- Slowing down your speech and pausing more often so that children can take in what you are telling them

- Using more visuals; for example, charting, diagramming, and sketching a visual representation to help children grasp what you are teaching

- Pausing often for rechecking. Stop and ask questions to help them rehearse information in short-term memory. For example you might say, "Who can tell me about . . ." or "When we read, how are we going to use . . . to help us . . .?"

Effective Workshop Instruction

An effective workshop session teaches, gives children time to practice, and then reinforces learning. This probably sounds a lot like any good teaching lesson, and you may wonder what makes a workshop a workshop. Workshop instruction gives children time to construct knowledge and develop understanding. Workshop instruction is framed by a short but powerful lesson and allows for groups of children to work through ideas together, to learn by discussing, attempting, writing, and sharing. They spend time talking through their thinking and developing knowledge through structured discussion. This is opposite of a more traditional lesson design, in which children sit at their desks, listen to the teacher, and then quietly and independently complete some type of practice activity. (See Figure 7.1.)

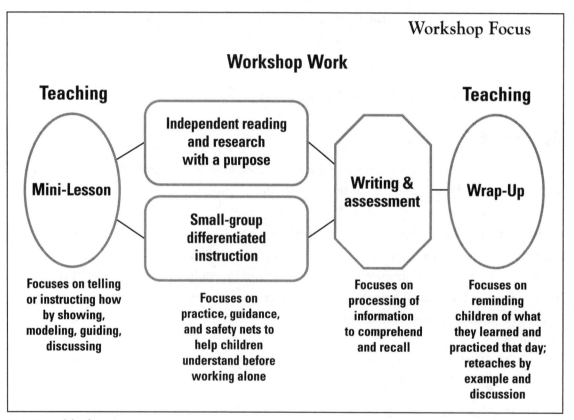

Figure 7.1: Workshop focus

The mini-lesson focuses on directly telling, or instructing how. Now, direct instruction is great, as long as you do something with it. That is why it is followed by guided practice, small-group teaching, and reteaching. So, the mini-lesson consists of focusing on one objective, taking children by the hand, and in a positive and supportive manner, *showing them how.*

The Content-Rich Reading & Writing Workshop

You want children to master the learning, so that is why you assess often and through quick and engaging participatory assessments. You will use paper-and-pencil assessments to check for understanding at planned intervals. These assessments might occur at the end of a unit, not during the day-to-day workshop.

Transparent teaching focuses on children constructing knowledge. Capitalize on the tension between your role and your students' roles in the workshop for the joint construction of knowledge. You push, and then the students may push back with new learning and ideas; you take this thinking in and then gently nudge the students on to learn more. Through focusing, nudging, and reframing, you will spiral student learning and help them make deep connections to content and reading.

Effective Design and Use of Time

An effective workshop includes the following elements:

- Mini-lesson
- Guided practice
- Discussion or sharing of learning
- Closure

By incorporating these four steps, you know that children have a chance of understanding what is going on in class and have the opportunity to learn and own new concepts. Transparent teaching occurs within each step. See the chart on page 110 for more information on how to incorporate the four steps into your classroom.

Workshop Design Step	What Makes This Transparent Teaching
Mini-Lesson: 15–20 minutes Occurs in the meeting area Each mini-lesson has these four parts: • Connection • Direct Instruction • Engagement • Wrap-Up	*Teacher Actions:* telling, showing, modeling, discussing The teacher carefully describes *one new concept*, models the concept, provides a visual reminder of the new information, and engages children with the new information. The focus is on a transfer of information from teacher to student, with emphasis on *what, why,* and *how.*
Guided Practice: 30 minutes Occurs in various places around the room: student desks, computer area, class library Students participate in various activities in class to complete work, including: • Reading from book sets • Reading assigned texts • Participating in reading groups • Writing about reading • Using graphic organizers • Recording information • Sharing information with peer partners Students use various materials in class to complete work, including the following: Book boxes Recording journals Content journals Vocabulary cards Whiteboards Graphic organizers Textbooks Nonfiction leveled texts Reference materials Library/trade books	*Teacher Actions:* conferring, assessing, teaching small-group sessions, reteaching *Student Actions:* reading, writing, discussing, thinking, keeping notes, recording The teacher participates in two main structures: teaching small groups or conferring and assessing. The teacher reinforces the *one* new concept taught, reteaches for understanding and ability in small groups or one-on-one by conferring (leads content lessons and guided reading), takes notes from student assessment, and chooses the focus for the discussion/sharing of learning.
Sharing of Learning: 8–9 minutes The class meets in the group meeting area and brings their books and notebooks with them.	*Teacher Actions:* During the guided practice the teacher listens for students who may be able to jump-start the sharing-of-learning time. These are children who are actively thinking through their work for the day. They may even be struggling a bit, as children can learn from one another as they see how someone solves a problem, applies a strategy, or even admits they don't know something. During the sharing, children listen to one another and reflect upon how their work related to the objective for the day. *Student Actions:* Children share their reading, research, writing, and learning with one another. They have the chance to speak in whole-group and small-group settings in order to become comfortable sharing and being the center of knowledge and information.
Closure: 1 minute Recap what occurred that day in the workshop and the objective of the lesson. Give a quick preview of what the class will be learning the next day.	*Teacher Actions:* telling, showing, discussing *Student Actions:* listening, thinking, sharing

Reflecting on Our Practice

There will be a point at which teaching transparently comes easily, so easily, in fact, that you may forget to stop and think about it any longer. When you reach this point, it is still important to reflect on your practice. By reflecting, you ensure that you are teaching well, that you are focused on the four essential elements of transparent teaching, and that you continue to focus on the *tell, show, tell* pattern. The best way to ensure that you are teaching transparently is to reflect on your practice.

You can reflect on your teaching practice by simply asking yourself a series of questions related to the steps of transparent teaching and then recording your thoughts. Focus on what you are actually doing and implementing, not what you wished, hoped, or dreamed would happen. When you focus on what you have actually implemented, you may be surprised at what you see in your teaching. For one thing, you have probably implemented more than you realize, and second, any adjustments you need to make will be less overwhelming because you can clearly define them. Figure 7.2 shows a sample reflection sheet. (See Appendix T, page 150, for a reproducible.).

After reflecting, the next step would be to incorporate more of the areas accidentally neglected in your teaching. This type of reflection helps us ensure that what we are implementing is what we intend to implement. Focus on answering these questions clearly and with examples. By doing so, you will help yourself grow and deepen your teaching practices.

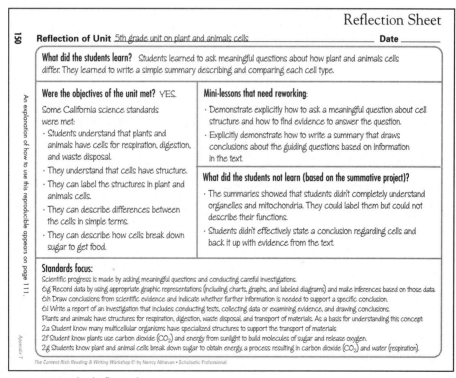

Figure 7.2 Completed reflection sheet

Focus on Transparent Teaching to Motivate

Our actions make or break our students' commitment and motivation to learn. I know, you might be thinking that this is just simply not true, that the children come to your classroom door each day either motivated or unmotivated. You probably have many experiences that pop into your mind to prove me wrong. I am sure these are all true, but if I didn't believe that I could make a difference in students' lives and believe that my actions make a difference in their desire to learn and to come to school each day, I would have trouble showing up to school each day! Most teachers I have met across the country share this sentiment: we *want* to make a difference, and for almost all students we *can*. Of course, this doesn't mean that we don't feel frustrated from time to time with our students' motivation and abilities.

It is true that I cannot change students who bring a lot of emotional baggage to the classroom, but I can support them. I can empower students to desire information, seek questions, thirst for answers, and find fascination in facts and tidbits of information.

Many children who land in our upper-grade classrooms with years of experience stumble at learning. They stumble at reading, they stumble at writing, and they stumble at spelling. After a while, they give up. When this happens, we may mistakenly assume that they know how to read, comprehend, and then express their ideas, and if they don't do so, then they don't care. We assign tasks for them to do, but we don't show them *how* to complete the tasks (Perry et al., 2006). Even when we do show them how, we don't break the steps down so that the children can own the process and the thinking.

One of the most important things we can do is make our teaching transparent and focused—and in every aspect of our teaching gently take their hands and show them how. Consider the old maxim of customer service: No question coming from a client or customer should be considered repetitious. I think this applies to teaching as well. It may have been the fiftieth time you've heard a particular question on a given day, but it's the first time that particular student has asked it. The student who is asking the question for the first time deserves the information and should hear it in a supportive voice even if you're sick of repeating yourself.

I've fallen into this trap. I thought that if I taught my heart out that somehow the world would mysteriously shift and the children would start coming to my classroom prepared and knowing what to do. Sometimes they did, but most often they did not. I realized that the children who came to my classroom knowing what to do really didn't need me to teach them— they tended to learn on their own. And then there were the other children—the ones who looked to me to help them. I had to get over the fact that I was answering the same question over and over again and realize it might be the first time a student was asking it!

Sometimes it is difficult to show children how year after year when in your mind you yearn for students to know so that you can move to grade level material and beyond. I know that my motivation lags from time to time. Just remember: it isn't the child's fault he doesn't know. You may need to slow your teaching down and show how. Students who know how to learn become motivated and can focus.

On-Ramp to Learning **Transparent Teaching**

- ◆ Telling is important; students shouldn't have to guess at what to do.
- ◆ Don't ask questions of students if it is information you want them to know, just *say it*. Ask questions later to check for understanding.
- ◆ Tell students what you are going to show them, show them, and then wrap up by telling them what you showed them.

    Tell them, show them, tell them what you showed them.

CHAPTER 8

Plan a Content-Based Unit of Study

How to Address Reading and Writing Strategies and Build Content Knowledge

To effectively teach a unit that simultaneously develops reading and writing strategies *and* content knowledge, begin by planning with the end in mind and then write an instructional road map that will get you to your destination.

Planning is the heart of good instruction. It helps you:

- Know where you are headed each academic school year

- Stay organized

- Ensure students are meeting state grade-level expectations

Keeping the End in Mind

It's essential to keep the outcome of the unit in mind as you plan. When you know what your students should know and be able to do at the end of the few weeks you spend on a unit, you will know how explicit to make your instruction. To do this, you begin with a focused objective and then write a plan that has a laser-like focus on meeting it (Wiggins & McTighe, 1998).

Crazy, you may think. What about all the other learning we are leaving out by focusing tightly on one or two big objectives? Don't worry—other learning will occur as students discover information and work with it. But at the end of a well-planned unit, at the very least you will reach the learning destination you set for students.

Planning is important because it keeps you organized. We are human and our brains are capable of paying attention to only a defined amount of information at any given time. By planning well we don't have to hold our instructional road map in our heads; we can glance at it as many times as we need to stay on track.

Defining a Learning Destination

Before writing an instructional road map, you need a clearly defined destination. Planning a learning destination begins with grade-level standards and ends with an eye on summative assessment data. What standards do you want to ensure students have met at the end of the unit? You also need to ensure that the unit responds to what students need to know for spring high-stakes tests (Jamentz, 2002).

Yes, high-stakes assessment data informs instruction from a programmatic viewpoint. It doesn't inform instruction as well as formative assessment, which is designed to give you indicators during the yearlong school journey about how the students are doing. While you may not agree with high-stakes testing and the subsequent accountability under No Child Left Behind legislative actions, there is one thing the numbers don't refute: the lack of preparedness of students living in poverty and students of color for high school. Not enough of our children are leaving our intermediate-grade classrooms ready for rigorous work (Brown, 2002; Graves, 2004).

Standards can be a learning destination. If the standard is written in terms of performance and states what a child should know and be able to do, it gives you an idea of what a child should be able to do at the end of a unit. Standards are often misinterpreted gatekeepers or inappropriate indicators of student success. While the sheer number of standards we are accountable for may be unwieldy, they are a helpful tool for determining what a student needs to learn. The standards also keep us all on the same page.

As an individual teacher, I have the professional responsibility to teach and scaffold instruction around the standards so that all students can master them. As a colleague or a part of a team, I have the professional responsibility to assess student progress, reflect on the process with colleagues, and brainstorm new avenues to ensure student success. But before we can do this, we need to truly understand what students are to know and do. We need to visualize what proficient students would look like in action and then work together to create powerful learning opportunities for all students in our classrooms.

Most standards are written as lists. In fact, the lists grow so long that they become overwhelming. It is helpful to think of the standard in terms of performances, or *what students will do*. Think about what student performance the standard exemplifies. If the standards you are working with are not written in terms of a performance, begin to think of them in terms of a performance by adding the phrase "Demonstrate the ability to" in front of the standard. For example if the standard is: "Monitor expository text for unknown words or words with novel meanings by using word, sentence, and paragraph clues to determine meaning" (California State Board of Education, 2007), add the phrase and it will state: *Demonstrate the ability to monitor expository text for unknown words or words with novel meanings **and** use word, sentence,* *and paragraph clues to determine meaning.* Rewording the sentence makes it easier to understand what students are to know and *do* and helps you focus on students rather than lists of information to cover.

Begin to think of standards as tools for developing conceptual understanding for children that other learning can hook onto. Children need connected, conceptual teaching and learning. Because many standards are written as long lists, it is essential to define which standards are overarching ideas and big concepts that other standards can fit inside. Consider, for example, the South Carolina fourth-grade science standard 4-2 for life science, organisms, and environments: "The student will demonstrate an understanding of the characteristics and patterns of behavior that allow organisms to survive in their own distinct environments (South Carolina Department of Education, 2007, p. 32). Indicators that fit within it include 4-2.2: "Explain how the characteristics of distinct environments influence the variety of organisms in each," and 4-2.5: "Explain how an organism's patterns of behavior are related to its environment." Instead of seeing the standards as separate and distinct skills or knowledge areas that students need to master, think about how each indicator fits inside the guiding standard. If a student is to understand that characteristics and behavior patterns allow organisms to survive in their environments, for example, he also has to understand that environments affect organisms and their behavior.

Our brains hook information together as we develop schemas and grow knowledge and understanding. Schemas are organizational units in our memory. When we develop knowledge about something, we develop a schema that encompasses the concepts connected to new learning. A schema grows like a web, and the knowledge of one domain is connected to knowledge of another domain (Anderson & Pearson, 1984). We don't have compartments in our memories where pieces of information sit individually; rather, they're interconnected. A schema provides a structure for new learning and allows us to construct new meaning from what we already know (Sousa, 2006; Zull, 2002).

Schemas are information storehouses that help us learn. When we connect children to learning at the beginning of a lesson and wake up their brains, we are priming them to connect new learning to prior learning. When thinking about content-area reading, children can comprehend text when they activate, or build, a schema that fits the information in the text. As their knowledge base develops in an area, or domain, children are able to organize information found in text more efficiently, make inferences to fill in gaps, and then elaborate on the reading. (Vacca, 2002).

Designing an Instructional Road Map

To use the content standards as an instructional road map, lay out the ones you want to teach in sequence over the course of a year and use them to guide your work through a unit of study (Akhavan, 2004). An instructional road map consists of these three parts:

1. Goal

2. Lesson guide sheet

3. Grading sheet or rubric

The goal of the unit is the learning destination, as defined by grade-level standards (discussed in the previous section), and a group of mini-lessons that are bound together by the goal. The unit is a cohesive, conceptual structure designed to build knowledge around a topic or area.

When planning the unit, consider these questions:

- What do you want students to do and or know by the end of unit (the learning destination)?

- What culminating assignment will they complete?

- How will you assess and grade the assignment?

- How will you scaffold your students with excellent instruction?

To make planning your unit of study easy, use the Curriculum Planning sheet shown in Figure 8.1. At the top of the sheet write the focus of the unit and the essential idea to be explored and learned by the students. (See Appendix U, page 151, for a reproducible.)

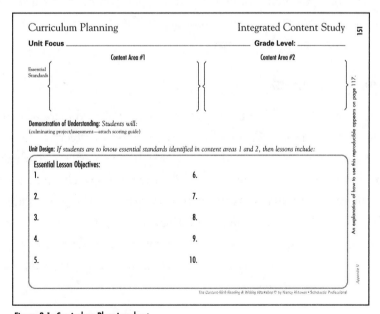

Figure 8.1: Curriculum Planning sheet

Choosing a Culminating Assignment

Before going on, it is important to think of the final project or assessment that you are expecting of students. It is pointless to have a learning destination if you don't know how students will show that they've reached it. You need to decide ahead of time because you will need to teach the steps in the process over the course of the unit (Wiggins & McTighe, 1998).

You may want to have students do a project rather than take a test. Projects stretch students beyond a test-taking format and help them learn facts and synthesize information. The following are some projects you might assign:

- Write an information report or other expository writing

- Keep a notebook and record information, reflection, and notes

- Create an investigation

- Make a timeline

- Create a work of historical fiction

- Analyze historical events and personalities and create an event board (like a storyboard)

- Complete a science or history board

- Finish an integrated assignment combining arts, science, or social studies

If you decide to have students complete a project, then you need to think about what you want students to do in response to the new information they are learning and how they are going to learn how to complete the project.

Assessing the Assignment

After plotting out a project and adding it to your instructional road map, it is time to decide how you want to grade the project. I find using a rubric to be an effective way to grade a project. You can also use a regular grading scale with cut scores, but if so, ensure that each step is spelled out so that your grading expectations are clear. One way to effectively grade a final project is by using an analytical rubric. An analytical rubric lists each step in the process and then assigns a weight (Kinsella, 2004). You can use the planning sheet to create the rubric and then weight the rubric according to the parts that you find most important. Rubrics aren't designed to be "gotcha" tools. They are designed to make teacher thinking and expectations clear so that all students know what to do to succeed.

During the content-based workshop, you will be meeting with students individually and in groups to assess their reading and to monitor and guide their understanding of and writing about the content. It is during this time that you can help children understand what is expected of them and how the rubric organizes information and expectations for them. Examples of how the work should look, or *how good is good enough*, should be in the room— on charts from mini-lessons and on walls filled with student thinking, writing, and group charts, (See Figure 8.2.)

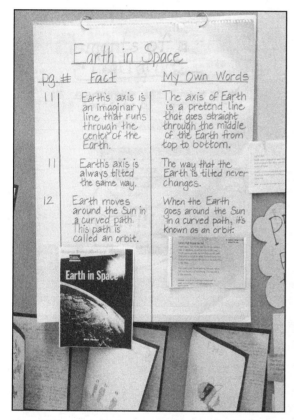 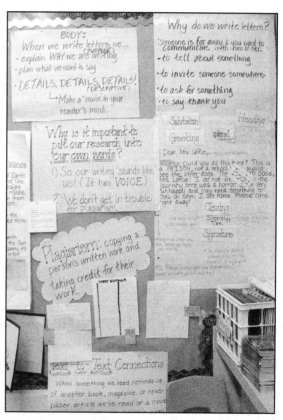

Figure 8.2: The walls in this classroom remind students of current learning and expectations.

One Rubric Example

Figure 8.3 is an example of a rubric from a fourth-grade social studies unit on the California gold rush. In this unit Cary Stolpestad assigns students a journal-writing project. Her students each developed a fictitious persona, taking care to be historically accurate in terms of their persona's skills, abilities, and attributes. The journal is a 10-page document with accurately dated entries that reflect the persona's experiences over one year in the gold rush era.

This rubric is scored using a numerical system. More important areas are weighted higher than other areas.

Scoring Fictitious Autobiographical Narrative

Description of Task	Score				Weight	Total score
1. Autobiography has at least four well-developed paragraphs, which include the details from the expectation sheet.	1	2	3	4	x 2 =	
2. Details regarding family, activities, occupation, and education are believable and based on information correct to the period in history.	1	2	3	4	x 2 =	
3. Gold rush vocabulary is incorporated in text. (See vocabulary list.)	1	2	3	4		
4. Narrative includes at least three references to research-based facts and historical events.	1	2	3	4		
5. Paper is handwritten neatly or typed. Paragraphs are indented, margins are 1" all around. Typed print size is no larger than 16, academic font is used (Arial, Times New Roman, Bookman).	1	2	3	4		
6. Gold rush persona development sheet is attached to narrative.	1	2	3	4		

Figure 8.3: Rubric for Scoring Fictitious Autobiographical Narrative

This rubric lists the parts of the investigation that the teacher expects the students to have in place and then weights each section. The steps are concrete and easy for students to visualize, as the teacher has modeled each step along the way. The analytical rubric is an effective way to mesh project-based assessment and a traditional grading practice.

How to Scaffold Learning With Excellent Instruction

Next you will need to brainstorm some of the lessons you will teach during the unit.

- What content lessons will you teach?

- What strategies or genre lessons will you teach?

To create your unit, begin by jotting down your ideas. You will use these notes to refine your expectations into a final project. Sometimes teachers ask me, "Well, how do I know what to teach?" Trust your instincts. If you are planning to teach a unit on weather patterns and the culminating project will be a written report with diagrams, then you are going to need to teach the processes of the water cycle, including evaporation, condensation, precipitation, and runoff; the daily and seasonal changes in weather conditions; and the conditions and effects of severe weather phenomena. But this is just the content children need to learn. They also need to learn how to write a scientific report, focus on facts, cite references, and create diagrams.

The expectations of *what* and *how* need to be listed both on the rubric and Curriculum Planning sheet, in specific terms. What do you expect the children to do: how many references do they need, how should these be formatted, how do they write the introductory paragraph, the details in the body? Of course you have your science textbooks to guide you, but if you take the time to reflect on the unit and the accompanying standards, you will have a pretty good idea of what you need to teach and in what order. The Curriculum Planning sheet is a recording sheet to sketch out the final project, develop the grading scale, organize teaching materials, and note your expectations for students' writing progress. By writing all of this down, you *ink what you think*.

You cannot assign students a report, persuasive essay, feature article, or summary without teaching those genres. You cannot expect children do to a good job on a timeline or an integrated project without explaining and modeling how to complete the project step by step. And when I say explain and model, I don't mean lecture and assign. Think of the understanding a student has to develop to complete an assignment independently. Consider how you want them to do the following:

- Approach the information and reading

- Take notes

- Finalize their writing, the artwork, or the timeline

- Complete any artwork or text features like timelines or any other graphic organizers

Planning a great unit isn't enough for children to understand *how*. All of this needs to be modeled by you. That way there won't be a lag between the children who already know how to tackle the assignment, or have someone at home to help them, and those who are working solo and don't have anyone to help.

To address the solo obstacle, break each task down into steps. Plan with a Backward Planning Sheet. The sheet helps you plot out a project over four to six weeks, beginning with the end and working toward the steps you need to take the first day. Keep your eye on the goal—what you want students to know and be able to do at the end of the unit of study. Plotting out your thinking ensures that your actual curriculum matches your intended curriculum. The road map also becomes a guideline to give students so they can pace themselves.

The planning sheet also gives you an avenue for you to reflect on your instruction. Midway through the unit it is helpful to stop and reflect on your progress. Consider these points: Have you taught what you intended to teach? Have you checked for student understanding—*Do they know what you taught? Did they actually learn it?* Remember that you cannot assume that because you taught something, the children learned it. You also cannot assume that if you planned something, you actually taught it. There have been days when I was teaching that I got so busy, I *never* got to lessons I considered to be important and essential for student learning.

See Figures 8.4–8.6 for samples of a completed Curriculum Planning sheet, Rubric Planning Sheet, and Backward Planning Sheet for a sixth-grade unit on Mesopotamia, Egypt, and Kush. (See Appendixes U–W, pages 151–153 for reproducibles.)

Transparent Instruction

To work at the speed of learning, your mini-lessons need to make your thinking transparent and help students understand the learning goals and strategies they are going to use to remember information and apply it to a project. Too often we expect students to receive information and then react to it by writing a paper, finishing an integrated project, or taking a test *before* we know they understand. Avoid *receive-and-react* teaching through transparent lessons. (Chapter 7 focuses on the steps to transparent teaching: setting the scene, making connections, telling the *what*, telling the *how*, assessing, and reteaching.)

Remember that the point of learning within a content-rich workshop is to read, think, and write about nonfiction texts and subject matter. Kids today can Google for facts. More important, they need to know what to do with that information. Plan well and teach well, and your students will learn the skills and habits of mind that will serve them well through a lifetime of learning.

Curriculum Planning

Integrated Content Study

Unit Focus _Early Civilizations: Mesopotamia, Egypt, and Kush_   **Grade Level:** _6th_

Content Area #1	Content Area #2
World History and Geography	**English Language Arts**
Essential Standards	

Essential Standards

WH 6.2 Students analyze the geographic, political, economic, religious, and social structure of the early civilizations of Mesopotamia, Egypt, and Kush.
WH 6.2.1 Trace the development of agricultural techniques that permitted the production of economic surplus and the emergence of cities as centers of cultures and power.
WH6.2.6 Describe the role of Egyptian trade in the eastern Mediterranean and Nile valley.

Comprehension and Analysis of Grade-Level-Appropriate Text
2.3 Connect and clarify main ideas by identifying their relationships to other sources and related topics.
2.4 Clarify an understanding of texts by creating outlines, logical notes, summaries, or reports.
Expository Critique
2.7 Make reasonable assertions about a text through accurate, supporting citations.

Unit Design: _If students are to know essential standards identified in content areas 1 and 2, then lessons include:_

Demonstration of Understanding: _Students will:_ Write an expository composition focused on description, explanation, comparison and contrast of each early civilization.

Essential Lesson Objectives:

1. Describe the key elements of ancient life in the civilizations of Mesopotamia, Egypt, and Kush.

2. Focus on how the Tigris and Euphrates Rivers aided or hindered the development of civilizations.

3. Understand the structures of city-states.

4. Identify key elements of agricultural development and its effects on power structures and daily life.

5. Discuss the differences and similarities between farmers and warriors and rulers.

6. Identify main ideas in chapter sections, and connect information to previously read material.

7. Write an outline for each early civilization.

8. Write a summary for each early civilization and include relevant details from anthology and supporting materials.

9. Create a Venn diagram comparing the daily life, agricultural development, and religious development of each civilization.

An explanation of how to use this reproducible appears on page 117.

Appendix U   **151**

Figure 8.4: Completed Curriculum Planning sheet

Expository Composition

Focus on description, explanation, and comparison and contrast of three early civilizations.

Civilizations: Mesopotamia, Egypt, and Kush

Description of Task	Score				Weight As appropriate	Total score
Project Criteria						
There are three to five sentences that state **the purpose of the paper and explain the three sections of the paper: description of each civilization, explanation of headings, and an overview of the comparison of each civilization.**	1	2	3	4	x 2 =	
There are **three sections to the paper:** a general description of each civilization, a comparison of three components of each civilization, and a conclusion.	1	2	3	4		
The **general description** of each civilization includes a general description of daily life, rise and fall of power, and period of existence.	1	2	3	4		
The paper discusses **three components of early civilization, which may include a description of** agricultural development and the relation to geography, explanation of daily life, description of political system, or other social structure presented in text.	1	2	3	4	x 2 =	
The **description of each component of early civilization includes two to three sentences comparing and contrasting that component to the same component of one other culture presented;** for example, daily life in Mesopotamia is compared and contrasted to daily life in Egypt.	1	2	3	4	x 2 =	
The **conclusion restates important information** comparing and contrasting the three civilizations.	1	2	3	4		

Figure 8.5: Completed rubric

Description of Task	Score				Weight As appropriate	Total score
Project Criteria						
The **sentences provide specific evidence** to **support the writer's understanding** of each component of early civilization.	1	2	3	4	x 2 =	
All **supporting sentences are relevant and provide specific evidence** from the text and/or supplementary materials.	1	2	3	4	x 2 =	
The sentences are written in a logical, easy-to-follow order.						
Proofreading Criteria						
1. Are all sentences complete? Do all sentences make sense?	1	2	3	4		
2. Do subjects and verbs agree?	1	2	3	4		
3. Are verbs written in correct tense?	1	2	3	4		
4. Does each sentence end with the correct punctuation?	1	2	3	4		
5. Do all sentences begin with a capital letter? Are all proper nouns and titles capitalized correctly?	1	2	3	4		
6. Are all words spelled correctly?	1	2	3	4		
Final Score						

Based on California Content Standards for World History and Geography and English Language Arts

Figure 8.5: continued

Backward Planning Sheet
6-Week Unit of Study

Unit Title/Focus: <u>Early Civilizations: Mesopotamia, Egypt, and Kush</u>

By the end of the unit, students will know and be able to: <u>Write an expository composition focused on</u>

<u>description, explanation, comparison and contrast.</u>

Week 1 Essential knowledge students need this week to reach the final goal:

know facts about Mesopotamia

Teaching Points:

Teach key elements of ancient life in Mesopotamia.

Teach Get the Gist sheet to aid in comprehension.

Demonstrate how to set up History notebooks: label specific headings.

Assessment:

Check History notebooks to ensure entries are complete and labeled correctly.

Collect two Get the Gist sheets and score for "gist" entries and identified vocabulary.

Week 2 Essential knowledge students need this week to reach the final goal:

know facts about Egypt

Teaching Points:

Teach key elements of ancient life in Egypt.

Teach Get the Gist sheet to aid in comprehension.

Demonstrate how to set up History notebooks: label specific headings.

Assessment:

Check History notebooks to ensure entries are complete and labeled correctly.

Collect two Get the Gist sheets and score for "gist" entries and identified vocabulary.

Week 3 Essential knowledge students need this week to reach the final goal:

compare facts about Mesopotamia and Egypt

Teaching Points:

Provide continued focus for notes in History notebooks: focus on comparing and contrasting how geography affects the rise and fall of civilizations.

Describe the three Egyptian kingdoms and how each shaped the civilization.

Teach how to compare and contrast daily life and political systems of Mesopotamia and Egypt using a web.

Assessment:

Check History notebooks to ensure entries are labeled correctly.

Students complete web comparing and contrasting the rise and fall of Mesopotamia and Egypt.

In each box, state the essential knowledge students must development,
list teaching points to focus lesson objectives, and state how learning will be assessed each week.

An explanation of how to use this reproducible appears on pages 121–122.

Figure 8.6: Completed Backward Planning Sheet

The Content-Rich Reading & Writing Workshop

Week 4 Essential knowledge students need this week to reach the final goal:

know facts about Kush

Teaching Points:

Teach key elements of ancient life in Kush.

Teach Get the Gist sheet to aid in comprehension.

Demonstrate how to set up History notebooks: focus on summarizing information.

Teach how to compare and contrast daily life and political system of Egypt and Kush using a Venn diagram.

Assessment:

Check History notebooks to ensure entries are complete and labeled correctly.

Collect two Get the Gist sheets and score for "gist" entries and identified vocabulary.

Assign one Venn diagram comparing and contrasting Kush and Egypt.

Week 5 Essential knowledge students need this week to reach the final goal:

compare facts about Mesopotamia, Egypt, and Kush

Teaching Points:

Provide continued focus for notes in History notebooks: select three sections to identify for expository essay.

Choose from sections discussed in each chapter.

Describe and summarize each section and research facts in text and supplementary materials.

Teach how to compare and contrast components of each civilization.

Teach how to cite a source accurately.

Use the Research/Application Protocol to help students complete the Research Organizer.

Teach expected section of the essay as described in the rubric.

Assessment:

Check History notebooks to ensure entries are complete and labeled correctly.

Assign Research Organizer focused on two components of each civilization.

Week 6 Essential knowledge students need this week to reach the final goal:

finish essay describing and comparing and contrasting selected components of each civilization

Teaching Points:

Teach each section as described in the rubric.

See rubric for details.

Collect rough draft of each essay section beginning on Monday and address learning gaps each day, Tuesday through Friday.

Assessment:

Collect rough draft of each section in rubric. Assess for effort. Assign final due date for completed project.

In each box, state the essential knowledge students must development,
list teaching points to focus lesson objectives, and state how learning will be assessed each week.

An explanation of how to use this reproducible appears on pages 121–122.

Figure 8.6: continued

On-Ramp to Learning ▶ **Create a Road Map**

◆ Start with where you want to end up, and plan what you need to teach to reach your learning destination.

◆ When you make your expectations transparent, students know what they need to do to learn and do well in class.

◆ Plan a unit by thinking of the culminating activity or test:
  – *What will students know and be able to do?*
  – *How will the expectations be scored?*
  – *How will you tell students about each step along the way?*

◆ *Ink* your ideas when you *think* of them. Don't leave anything to chance.

Appendixes

Contents

Reproducibles

Book List

Recommended supplementary materials for teaching content at various levels

Publisher	Collection Title	Reading Level
Benchmark Education	Themed-Level Text *Earth and Space* *Our Physical World* *Plants* *Habitats* *The Human Body* *Government and Citizenship* *The Environment* *Invention and Technology*	Grade 3
	Themed-Level Text *United States History* *Regions of the United States* *Native Americans* *Geography* *Civilizations of the Americas* *Earth and Space* *Light and Sound* *Electricity and Magnetism*	Grade 4
	Themed-Level Text *Water and Weather* *Rocks and Minerals* *The Human Body* *Plants and Animals* *Chemistry* *United States History* *American Revolution* *Early Explorers* *The Constitution* *The Civil War*	Grade 5
Heinemann-Raintree	Themed-Level Text *Early River Civilizations* *Ancient Civilizations* *Settling America* *10th Century History* *The Renaissance* *World Geography*	Grade 6
	Science *Amazing Nature* *Animal Groups* *Building Blocks of Matter* (not leveled) *Using Materials* *Machines in Action*	Guided Reading levels P–R
	Science *Sea Creatures* *Living Habitats* *Body Matters* *Classifying Living Things* *Tabletop Scientist* *Earth's Processes* *Disasters in Nature*	Guided Reading levels S–U

The Content-Rich Reading & Writing Workshop © by Nancy Akhavan • Scholastic Professional

Book List

Recommended supplementary materials for teaching content at various levels

Publisher	Collection Title	Reading Levels
Heinemann-Raintree	Science *The Life of Plants* *Wild Predators* *Hidden Life* *Adapted for Success* *Animals Under Threat* *Animal Kingdom* *Life Processes* *Measuring the Weather* *Rocks and Minerals* *The Universe* *Fantastic Forces* *Essential Energy* *Chain Reactions* (not leveled) *Cell Life*	Guided Reading levels T–Z
	Social Studies *Continents* *Regions of the USA* *State Studies* *Mapping Earthforms* *First Guide to Government* (not leveled) *Picture the Past* *History Opens Windows*	Guided Reading levels O–T
	Social Studies *Map Readers* *Biomes Atlases* *Planet Under Pressure* *Regions of the World* *Our Government* *American Adventure* *Voice of Freedom* *13 Colonies* *Making a New Nation* *Hands-On Ancient History* *Everyday Economics*	Guided Reading levels U–Z
Teacher Created Materials	Social Studies *World Cultures Through Time* *Early America* *Expanding and Preserving the Union* *Biographies*	Grades 3–5
National Geographic	Science *Life Science* *The Human Body* *Earth Science* *Physical Science*	Guided Reading levels S–X
	Social Studies *Civilizations Past to Present* *American Communities Across Time* *Voices From America's Past*	Guided Reading levels O–T
	Social Studies *World Cultures* *World History* *World Explorers* *Seeds of Change in American History*	Target grade levels 5–8

The Content-Rich Reading & Writing Workshop © by Nancy Akhavan • Scholastic Professional

Reading Log

Name _____ Date _____

In/out	Book title	Author	Pages read #	Parent signature

An explanation of how to use this reproducible appears on page 35.

Appendix B

Name ——————— Date ——————— Vocabulary Log—Words to Learn

Book Title ———————

Word	Self-evaluation * I know it * I don't know it	Sentence and page #	Synonym for the word

An explanation of how to use this reproducible appears on page 36.

Name _____ **Date** _____

Title: _____

Get the Gist
(Look at the text features and scan the text.)

Important Ideas
(Summarize key points.)

Important Vocabulary
(Bold words, important terms)

An explanation of how to use this reproducible appears on page 38.

The Content-Rich Reading & Writing Workshop © by Nancy Akhavan • Scholastic Professional

Appendix D

Name _____ **Date** _____

Title: _____

Section Heading
Write it here.

Important Fact #1	Important Fact #2	Important Fact #3
Supporting Details Write them here.	**Supporting Details** Write them here.	**Supporting Details** Write them here.

The Content-Rich Reading & Writing Workshop © by Nancy Akhavan • Scholastic Professional

An explanation of how to use this reproducible appears on page 39.

Web

Name _____

Title: _____

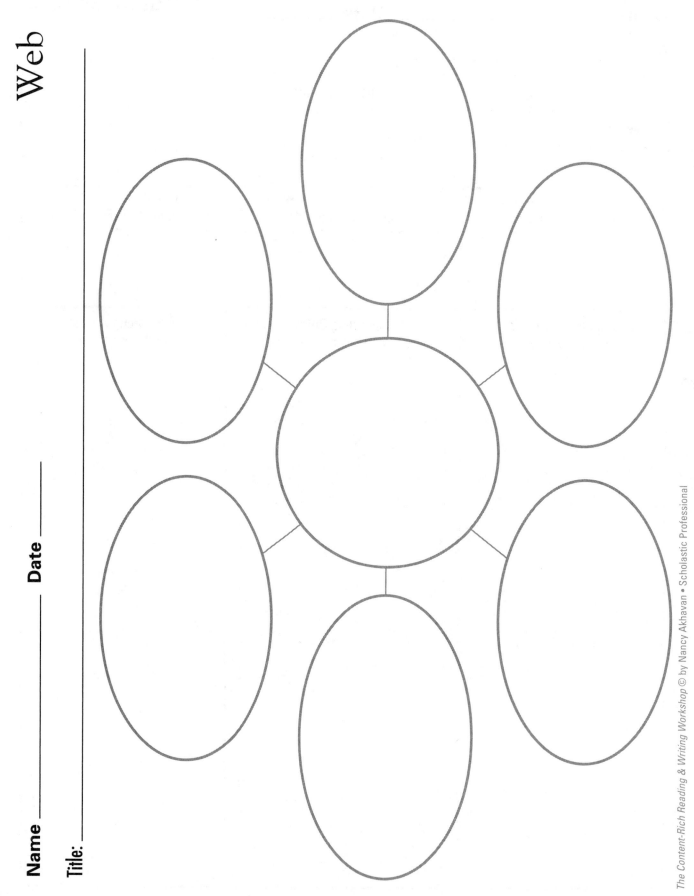

An explanation of how to use this reproducible appears on page 47.

The Content-Rich Reading & Writing Workshop © by Nancy Akhavan • Scholastic Professional

Name _____ **Date** _____ Connect This Idea!

Title: _____

Author: _____

Paraphrase what the book says: _____

_____

_____

_____

_____

_____

_____

_____

_____

What <u>connection</u> can I make to this information?

An explanation of how to use this reproducible appears on pages 48–49.

The Content-Rich Reading & Writing Workshop © by Nancy Akhavan • Scholastic Professional

Name _____ **Date** _____ # Text Feature Sheet

Title: _____

Author: _____

+--+
| Text Features |
| |
| pictures   diagrams   tables |
| |
| index   graphs   bold words |
| |
| glossary   captions   maps |
| |
| Other: _____ |
+--+

Information I noticed: _____

_____

_____

_____

_____

_____

_____

_____

An explanation of how to use this reproducible appears on pages 49–51.

The Content-Rich Reading & Writing Workshop © by Nancy Akhavan • Scholastic Professional

Appendix H

Problem-Solution

Title: _____ Author: _____

Problem

Solution

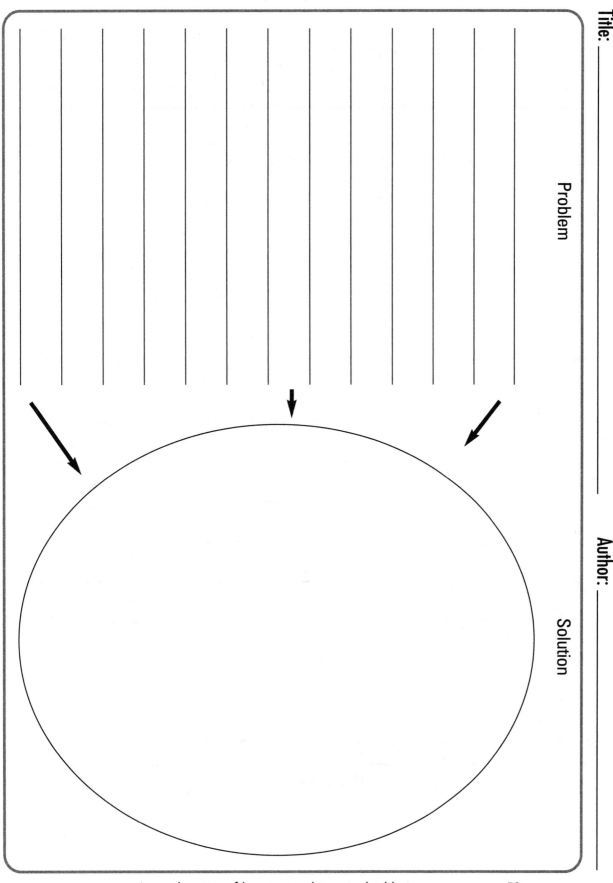

An explanation of how to use this reproducible appears on page 52.

Name _____ **Date** _____

Identifying
Important Information

Title: _____

Author: _____ pp #: _____

In the section labeled: _____,
the following facts were presented (continue on back if needed):

From the information, 2–3 important facts include:

1) _____

_____

_____

2) _____

_____

_____

3) _____

_____

_____

Vocabulary

The Content-Rich Reading & Writing Workshop © by Nancy Akhavan • Scholastic Professional

Asking Questions Bookmark

PAUSE & CHECK	PAUSE & CHECK	PAUSE & CHECK
Step 1) Ask yourself: "Do I understand what I just read?" If you answered yes: Keep reading If you answered no: Reread the section	Step 1) Ask yourself: "Do I understand what I just read?" If you answered yes: Keep reading If you answered no: Reread the section	Step 1) Ask yourself: "Do I understand what I just read?" If you answered yes: Keep reading If you answered no: Reread the section
Step 2) If you understand what you read, then ask yourself: "What is this section or page about?" (Describe it to yourself.) AND "What details support the main idea?" (List them in your head.) AND When did this occur?" (Check the dates/time/period in history.)	Step 2) If you understand what you read, then ask yourself: "What is this section or page about?" (Describe it to yourself.) AND "What details support the main idea?" (List them in your head.) AND When did this occur?" (Check the dates/time/period in history.)	Step 2) If you understand what you read, then ask yourself: "What is this section or page about?" (Describe it to yourself.) AND "What details support the main idea?" (List them in your head.) AND When did this occur?" (Check the dates/time/period in history.)
Step 3) Now, tell yourself the gist of the section. ## Keep reading!	Step 3) Now, tell yourself the gist of the section. ## Keep reading!	Step 3) Now, tell yourself the gist of the section. ## Keep reading!

Cut the bookmarks apart. Have students use a bookmark while reading to aid comprehension.

The Content-Rich Reading & Writing Workshop © by Nancy Akhavan • Scholastic Professional

Appendix K An explanation of how to use this reproducible appears on page 54.

Name _____ **Date** _____

Title: _____ **Author:** _____

Section Heading: _____

Picture It!

What do I see in my mind when reading this section?

THINK:
How does what I see help me understand?

_____

_____

_____

OR:
How does this image I see relate to the beginning, middle, or end of the text?

_____

_____

OR:
Thinking of the image, can I predict the main idea, or end of the text?

_____

_____

_____

An explanation of how to use this reproducible appears on pages 55–56.

The Content-Rich Reading & Writing Workshop © by Nancy Akhavan • Scholastic Professional

Appendix L

Write a summary of the information presented. Address the following:
- Topic
- Important facts
- Supporting details
- Relevance of information

Remember to introduce the piece and provide a conclusion.

Book title/section: _____

Author: _____

Summary: _____

_____

_____

_____

_____

_____

_____

_____

_____

_____

_____

_____

_____

_____

_____

_____

_____

_____

_____

An explanation of how to use this reproducible appears on pages 56.

Information Frame

Name _____ **Date** _____

Work in a group. Follow the directions, and then write your answers in a notebook or on the reproducible sheet. When you are done, write a short summary *on your own* using the words and topic sentence from the group work.

Article or book title: _____

_____

Author: _____

Group work—Step 1:
Identify the main idea of the text. Write it in sentence form in your notebook: *The main idea is . . .*
You may have to write several sentences.

Group work—Step 2:
Cross out any words in the main idea sentences that aren't important to understanding the focus of the main idea. Copy the remaining words in a chart. One column lists *people, items, or things* and the other column lists *actions or events*.

People/Items/Things	Actions/Events

Group work—Step 3:
Choose a word or phrase to replace the list of people/items/things and choose a word or phrase to replace the list of actions/events.

People/Items/Things	Actions/Events

OR

People/Items/Things	Actions/Events

Group work—Step 4:
Write a topic sentence for your summary using the words you brainstormed from your list.

Individual work—Step 5:
Use the topic sentence to write a summary of the article, book, or text you read. You will write it on your own and then compare your ideas and thinking with those of other members of your group.
Remember—this information frame helps you "own" your ideas and work, which makes the writing easier!

An explanation of how to use this reproducible appears on page 57.

The Content-Rich Reading & Writing Workshop © by Nancy Akhavan • Scholastic Professional

Appendix N

Name _____ **Date** _____ Reading Response

Book title: _____ **Author:** _____

In the introduction of the text, the following points were made:

_____

_____

_____

_____

The middle of the text stated the following information:

_____

_____

_____

_____

_____

_____

_____

The concluding points of the text stated the following:

_____

_____

_____

_____

_____

On a sheet of paper, write a summary of the text using this information. Remember to introduce the text and author and provide a conclusion.

An explanation of how to use this reproducible appears on page 58.

Name _____ **Date** _____

Title: _____

Author: _____ pp #: _____

Concept # 1	Concept # 2
List **similarities** between the two concepts.	List **differences** between the two concepts.

An explanation of how to use this reproducible appears on page 59.

The Content-Rich Reading & Writing Workshop © by Nancy Akhavan • Scholastic Professional

Appendix P

Name _____ **Date** _____

Two-Column Notes:
Main Idea & Details

Title: _____

Author: _____

Page #	Main Idea	Supporting Details

An explanation of how to use this reproducible appears on page 60.

The Content-Rich Reading & Writing Workshop © by Nancy Akhavan • Scholastic Professional

Appendix Q

147

Name _____ **Date** _____

Title: _____

Author: _____

Two-Column Notes

Get the Gist

Write what the text actually states. Include page numbers.	Write the gist of the text. Jot a note about what you think it is mainly about.

An explanation of how to use this reproducible appears on page 61.

The Content-Rich Reading & Writing Workshop © by Nancy Akhavan • Scholastic Professional

Appendix R

Name _____ Date _____

Research Organizer

Research Project: _____ Due Date: _____

Section or Category: _____

Page #	Resource Information	Fact/Information	Significance
	Title		
	Author		
	Reference or URL		
	Title		
	Author		
	Reference or URL		
	Title		
	Author		
	Reference or URL		

An explanation of how to use this reproducible appears on page 101.

Reflection Sheet

Reflection of Unit _____   **Date** _____

What did the students learn?

Were the objectives of the unit met?

Mini-lessons that need reworking:

What did the students not learn (based on the summative project)?

Standards focus:

An explanation of how to use this reproducible appears on page 111.

Appendix T

Curriculum Planning

Integrated Content Study

Unit Focus: _____   **Grade Level:** _____

Essential
Standards

Content Area #1

Content Area #2

Demonstration of Understanding: _Students will:_
(culminating project/assessment—attach scoring guide)

Unit Design: _If students are to know essential standards identified in content areas 1 and 2, then lessons include:_

Essential Lesson Objectives:

1.

2.

3.

4.

5.

6.

7.

8.

9.

10.

An explanation of how to use this reproducible appears on page 117.

Rubric Planning Sheet

Scoring project _____
(Title here)

Description of Task Write indicator based on explanation of expectations on project outline	Score	Weight As appropriate	Total score
1.	1　2　3　4	x 1 = or x 2 =	
2.	1　2　3　4	x 1 = or x 2 =	
3.	1　2　3　4	x 1 = or x 2 =	
4.	1　2　3　4	x 1 = or x 2 =	
5.	1　2　3　4	x 1 = or x 2 =	
6.	1　2　3　4	x 1 = or x 2 =	

An explanation of how to use this reproducible appears on pages 119–120.

The Content-Rich Reading & Writing Workshop © by Nancy Akhavan • Scholastic Professional

Backward Planning Sheet
4-Week Unit of Study

Unit Title/Focus: _____

By the end of the unit, students will know and be able to: _____

Week 1 Essential knowledge students need this week to reach the final goal:

Teaching Points:

Assessment:

Week 2 Essential knowledge students need this week to reach the final goal:

Teaching Points:

Assessment:

Week 3 Essential knowledge students need this week to reach the final goal:

Teaching Points:

Assessment:

Week 4 Essential knowledge students need this week to reach the final goal:

Teaching Points:

Assessment:

In each box, state the essential knowledge students must develop,
list teaching points to focus lesson objectives, and state how learning will be assessed each week.

An explanation of how to use this reproducible appears on pages 121–122.

References

Afflerbach, P. (2000). Verbal reports and protocol analysis. In M. L. Kamil, P. B. Mosenthal, P. D. Pearson, & R. Barr (Eds.), *Handbook of reading research*. Mahwah, NJ: Lawrence Erlbaum Associates.

Akhavan, N. (2004). *How to align literacy instruction, assessment, and standards and achieve results you never dreamed possible.* Portsmouth, NH: Heinemann.

Akhavan, N. (2006). *Help! My kids don't all speak English: How to set up a language workshop in your linguistically diverse classroom.* Portsmouth, NH: Heinemann.

Akhavan, N. (2007). *Accelerated vocabulary instruction: Strategies for closing the achievement gap for all students.* New York: Scholastic.

Allington, R. (2001). *What really matters for struggling readers.* New York: Addison Wesley.

Alvarez, D., & Mehan, H. (2004). Providing educational opportunities for underrepresented students. In D. Lapp (Ed.), *Teaching all the children.* New York: Guilford Press.

Alvermann, D. E., Fitzgerald, J., & Simpson, M. (2006). Teaching and learning in reading. In P. A. Alexander & P. H. Winne (Eds.), *Handbook of educational psychology* (pp. 427–455). Mahwah, NJ: Lawrence Erlbaum Associates.

Anderson, R. C., & Pearson, P. D. (1984). A schema-theoretic view of basic processes in reading comprehension. In P. D. Pearson, R. Barr, M. L. Kamil, & P. Mosenthal (Eds.), *Handbook of reading research* (pp. 255–292). Mahwah, NJ: Lawrence Erlbaum Associates.

Arthaud, T. J., & Goracke, T. (2006). Implementing a structured story web and outline strategy to assist struggling readers. *The Reading Teacher, 59,* 581–586.

Atwell, N. (2007). *The reading zone: How to help kids become skilled, passionate, habitual, critical readers.* Portsmouth, NH: Heinemann.

Baker, L., & Brown, A. L. (2002). Metacognitive skills and reading. In P. D. Pearson, R. Barr, M. L. Kamil, & P. Mosenthal (Eds.), *Handbook of reading research.* (pp. 353–394). Mahwah, NJ: Lawrence Erlbaum Associates.

Barton, P. E. (2004.) "Why does the gap persist?" *Educational leadership, 62,* 9–13.

Beres, S. (2005). *Energy resources around the world.* Pelham, NY: Benchmark Education Co.

Block, C. C., Schaller, J. L., Joy, J. A., & Gaine, P. (2002). Process-based comprehension instruction: Perspectives of four reading educators. In C. C. Block & M. Pressley (Eds.), *Comprehension instruction: Research-based best practices* (pp. 42–61). New York: Guilford.

Bransford, J. D., Vye, N., Stevens, R., Kuhl, P., Schwartz, D., Bell, P. et al. (2006). Learning theories and education: Toward a decade of synergy. In P. A. Alexander & P. H. Winne (Eds.), *Handbook of educational psychology* (pp. 209–244). Mahwah, NJ: Lawrence Erlbaum Associates.

Brophy, J. (2006). Observational research on generic aspects of classroom teaching. In P. A. Alexander & P. H. Winne (Eds.), *Handbook of educational psychology* (pp. 2755–2780). Mahwah, NJ: Lawrence Erlbaum Associates.

Brown, R. (2002). Straddling two worlds: Self-directed comprehension instruction for middle schoolers. In C. C. Block & M. Pressley (Eds.), *Comprehension instruction: Research-based best practices* (pp. 336–350). New York: Guilford Press.

Cabral, E. (2006, September 18). The Great Divide. *Scholastic News,* pp. 4–5.

California State Board of Education. English language arts standards, grade four. Retrieved August 22, 2007, from http://www.cde.ca.gov/be/st/ss/enggrade4.asp.

Chall, J. S. (2000). *The academic achievement challenge: What really works in the classroom?* New York: Guilford Press.

Chall, J. S., & Jacobs, V. A. (2003). Poor children's fourth-grade slump. *American Educator, 27.* Retrieved 12/23/07 from http://www.aft.org/pubs-reports/american_educator/spring2003/chall.html.

Dole, J., Duffy, G., Roehler, L., & Pearson, P. D. (1991). Moving from the old to the new: Research on reading comprehension instruction. *Review of Educational Research, 61,* 239–264.

Dollar coins (2006, December 18). *Scholastic News,* p. 2.

Donovan, S. (2004). *Rosa Parks.* Chicago: Heinemann-Raintree.

Dreher, M. J. (2002). Children searching and using information: A critical part of comprehension. In C.C. Block & M. Pressley (Eds.), *Comprehension instruction: Research-based best practices* (pp. 289–304). New York: Guilford Press.

Duffy, G. G. (2002). The case for direct explanation of strategies. In C. C. Block & M. Pressley (Eds.), *Comprehension instruction: Researched-based best practices* (pp. 28–41). New York: Guilford Press.

Duke, N. K., & Pearson, P. D. (2002). Effective practices for developing reading comprehension. In A. E. Farstrup & S. J. Samuels (Eds.), *What research has to say about reading instruction, third edition* (pp. 205–242). Newark: DE: International Reading Association.

Earle, S. A. (2000). *Sea Critters.* New York: Scholastic.

El-Dinary, P. B. (2002). Challenges of implementing transactional strategies instruction for reading comprehension. In C. C. Block & M. Pressley (Eds.), *Comprehension instruction: Researched-based best practices* (pp. 201–218). New York: Guilford Press.

Farstrup, A. E. (2002). There is more to effective reading instruction than research. In A. E. Farstrup & S. J. Samuels (Eds.). *What research has to say about reading instruction* (3rd ed., pp. 1–7). Newark, DE: International Reading Association.

Fisher, J. B., Schumaker, J. B., & Deshler, D. D. (2002). Improving the reading comprehension of at-risk adolescents. In C. C. Block & M. Pressley (Eds.), *Comprehension instruction: Research-based best practices* (pp. 361–364). New York: Guilford Press.

Fountas, I. C., & Pinnell, G. S. (1996). *Guided reading: Good first reaching for all students.* Portsmouth, New Hampshire: Heinemann.

Fountas, I. C., & Pinnell, G. S. (2006). *Teaching for comprehending and fluency: Thinking, talking, and writing about reading, K–8.* Portsmouth, NH: Heinemann.

Freeman, D., & Freeman, Y. (1998). *ESL/EFL teaching: Principles for success.* Portsmouth, NH: Heinemann.

Freeman, D., & Freeman, Y. (2003). Teaching English learners to read: Learning or acquisition? In G. G. Garcia (Ed.), *English learners: Reaching the highest level of English literacy* (pp. 34–54). Newark, DE: International Reading Association.

Fuel for thought (2006, November 13–27). *Scope,* pp. 12–15.

Furgang, K. (2004). *Building Bridges.* Pelham, NY: Benchmark Education Co.

Garfman, C. (2006, November 13–27). Fuel for thought. *Scholastic Scope, 55,* pp. 12–14.

Gaskins, R. W. (1996). "That's just how it was": The effect of issue-related emotional involvement on reading comprehension. *Reading Research Quarterly, 31,* 386–405.

Giblin, J. C. (2004). *Secrets of the Sphinx.* New York: Scholastic.

Going the Distance. (2007, February). *Super Science, 18,* pp. 6–9.

Grant, D. A., Stern, I. B., & Everett, F. G. (1979). *Periodontics: In the tradition of Orban and Gottlieb* (5th ed.). St. Louis, MO: C. V. Mosby Company.

Graesser, A. C., McNamara, D. S., & Louwerse, M. M. (2003). What do readers need to learn in order to process coherence relations in narrative and expository text? In A. P. Sweet & C. E. Snow (Eds.), *Rethinking reading comprehension.* New York: Guilford Press.

Graves, M. (2004). Theories and constructs that have made a significant difference in adolescent literacy—but have the potential to produce still more positive results. In T. L. Jetton & J. A. Dole (Eds.), *Adolescent literacy research and practice* (pp. 433–452). New York: Guilford Press.

Grigg, W., Donahue, P., & Dion, G. (2007). *The nation's report card: 12th grade reading and mathematics 2005.* (NCES 2007–468). U.S. Department of Education, National Center for Education Statistics. Washington DC: U.S. Government Printing Offices.

Guthrie, J. T. (2003). Concept-oriented reading instruction. In A. P. Sweet & C. E. Snow (Eds.), *Rethinking reading comprehension* (pp. 115–140). New York: Guilford Press.

Guthrie, J. T., & Wigfield, A. (2000). Engagement and motivation in reading. In P. A. Alexander & P. H. Winne (Eds.), *Handbook of educational psychology.* Mahwah, NJ: Lawrence Erlbaum Associates.

Hansen, J., & Pearson, P. D. (1983). An instructional study: Improving the inferential comprehension of good and poor fourth-grade readers. *Journal of Educational Psychology, 75,* 821–829.

Harvey, S. (1998). *Nonfiction matters: Reading, writing, and research in grades 3–8.* Portland, Maine: Stenhouse.

Hasbrouck, J., & Tindal, G. A. (2006). Oral reading fluency norms: A valuable assessment tool for reading teachers. *The Reading Teacher, 59,* 636–644.

Hiebert, E. H. (2002). Standards, assessments, and text difficulty. In A. E. Farstrup & S. J. Samuels (Eds.), *What research has to say about reading instruction* (pp. 337–369). Newark, DE: International Reading Association.

Hirsch, E. D. (2003). Reading comprehension requires knowledge—of words and the world. *American Educator*, 27, 10–13, 16–22, 28–29, 48.

Hirsch, E. D., Jr. (2006). *The knowledge deficit: Closing the shocking education gap for American students.* Boston: Houghton Mifflin.

Investigate the giant squid. Retrieved on 7/24/07 from http://teacher.scholastic.com/activities/explorations/squid/.

Jamentz, K. (2002). *Instructional leadership to support standards-based practice.* San Francisco, CA: WestEd.

Jetton, T. L., & Alexander, P. A. (2004). Domains, teaching and literacy. In T. L. Jetton, & J. A. Dole (Eds.), *Adolescent literacy research and practice.* New York: Guilford Press.

Kinsella, K. (2004). *Academic writing scaffolds for mixed-ability content area classrooms.* Presented on September 24, 2004, Clovis, CA.

Klinger, J. K., & Vaughn, S. (2004). Strategies for struggling second-language readers. In T. L. Jetton & J. A. Dole (Eds.), *Adolescent literacy research and practice,* (pp. 183–209). New York: Guilford Press.

Knipper, K. J., & Duggan, T. J. (2006). Writing to learn across the curriculum: Tools for comprehension in content area classes. *The Reading Teacher*, 59, 462–470.

Krashen, S. (2003). *Explorations in language acquisition and use.* Portsmouth, NH: Heinemann.

Krathwohl, D. R. (2002.) A revision of Bloom's taxonomy: An overview. *Theory Into Practice*, 41, 212–218.

Lee, J., Grigg, W. S., & Donahue, P. L. (2007). *The nation's report card: Reading 2007.* Retrieved October 9, 2007, from http://nces.ed.gov/nationsreportcard/pubs/main2007/2007496.asp

Livingston, A., & Wirt, J. (2005). *The condition of education 2005 in brief* (NCES 2005-095) U.S. Department of Education, National Center for Education Statistics. Washington, DC: US Government Printing Office.

Long, D. L., Wilson, J., Hurley, R., & Pratt, C. S. (2006). Assessing text representations with recognition: The interaction of domain knowledge and text coherence. *Journal of Experimental Psychology: Learning, Memory and Cognition*, 32, 816–827.

Lubliner, S. (2004.) Help for struggling upper-grade elementary readers. *The Reading Teacher*, 7, 430–438.

Lyons, C.A. (2003). *Teaching struggling readers: How to use brain-based research to maximize learning.* Portsmouth, NH: Heinemann.

Mayer, R. E., & Wittrock, M. C. (2006). Problem solving. In P. A. Alexander & P. H. Winne (Eds.), *Handbook of educational psychology* (pp. 287–303). Mahwah, NJ: Lawrence Erlbaum Associates.

McKee, J., & Ogle, D. (2005). *Integrating instruction: Literacy and science.* New York: Guilford Press.

Meanley, E. (2007, April 9). Indy-pendent fuel. *Scholastic Scope*, 55, pp. 12–13.

Moore, D. W., Readence, J. E., & Rickelman, R. J. (1989). *Prereading activities for content area reading and learning,* (2nd ed.) Newark: DE: International Reading Association.

Murphy, P. K. & Mason, L. (2006). Changing knowledge and beliefs. In P. A. Alexander & P. H. Winne (Eds.) *Handbook of Educational Psychology,* (2nd ed., pp. 305–326). Mahwah, NJ: Lawrence Erlbaum, Associates.

Nagy, W., Berninger, V. W., & Abbot, R. D. (2006). Contributions of morphology beyond phonology to literacy outcomes of upper elementary and middle school students. *Journal of Educational Psychology*, 98, 134–147.

National Center for Education Statistics. (2004). Percentage of students, by reading achievement level, grade 4: 1992–2003. *The Nation's Report Card: Reading.* Washington DC: National Center for Education Statistics, Institute of Education Sciences, U.S. Department of Education. Retrieved August 23, 2007, from http://nces.ed.gov/nationsreportcard/reading/results2003/natachieve-g4.asp.

National Institute of Child Health and Human Development, NICHHD. (2000). *Report of the National Reading Panel. Teaching students to read: An evidence-based assessment of the scientific research literature on reading and its implications for reading instruction* (NIH Publication No. 00-4769). Washington, DC: U.S. Government Printing Office.

National Writing Project & Nagin, C. (2006). *Because writing matters: Improving student writing in our schools.* San Francisco: Jossey-Bass.

Neufeld, P. (2005). Comprehension instruction in content area classes. *The Reading Teacher*, 59, 302–312.

Neuman, S. B., & Celano, D. (2006). The knowledge gap: Implications for leveling the playing field for low-income and middle-income students. *Reading Research Quarterly*, 41 176–201.

Nokes, J. D., & Dole, J. A. (2004). Helping adolescent readers through explicit strategy instruction. In T. L. Jetton & J. A. Dole (Eds.), *Adolescent Literacy Research and Practice* (pp. 162–182). New York: Guilford Press.

Ogle, D., & Blachowicz, C. L. Z. (2002). Beyond literature circles: Helping students comprehend informational texts. In C. C. Block & M. Pressley (Eds.), *Comprehension instruction: Research-based best practices* (pp. 259–274). New York: Guilford Press.

Olsen, L., & Jaramillo, A. (1999). *Turning the tides of exclusion: A guide for educators and advocates for immigrant students.* Oakland, CA: California Tomorrow.

Pappas, C. C. (2006). The informational book genre: Its role in integrated science literacy research and practice. *Reading Research Quarterly, 41*, 226–250.

Payne, E. (1964). *The pharaohs of ancient Egypt.* New York: Random House.

Pearson, P. D., & Duke, N. K. (2002). Comprehension instruction in the primary grades. In C. C. Block & M. Pressley (Eds.), *Comprehension Instruction: Research-based best practices,* (pp. 247–258). New York: Guilford Press.

Pearson, P. D., & Raphael, T. E. (2003). Toward a more complex view of balance in the literacy curriculum. In L.M. Morrow, L.B. Gambrell, & M. Pressley (Eds.), *Best practices in literacy instruction.* New York: Guilford Press.

Perry, B. *How the brain learns best: Easy ways to gain optimal learning in the classroom by activating different parts of the brain.* Retrieved from October 21, 2007, from http://teacher.scholastic.com/professional/bruceperry/brainlearns.htm.

Perry, N. E., Turner, J. C., & Meyer, D. (2006). Classrooms as contexts for motivating learning. In P. A. Alexander & P. H. Winne (Eds.), *Handbook of educational psychology,* (pp. 327–348). Mahwah, NJ: Lawrence Erlbaum Associates.

Pressley, M. (2000). What should comprehension instruction be the instruction of? In M. L. Kamil, P. B. Mosenthal, D. Pearson, & R. Barr. (Eds.), *Handbook of reading research.* Mahwah, NJ: Lawrence Erlbaum Associates.

Pressley, M. (2002a). Metacognition and self-regulated comprehension. In A. E. Farstrup, & S. J. Samuels (Eds.), *What research has to say about reading instruction* (pp. 291–309). Newark, DE: International Reading Association.

Pressley, M. (2002b). *Reading instruction that works: The case for balanced teaching* (2nd ed.). New York: Guilford Press.

Pressley, M. (2004). The need for research on secondary literacy education. In T. L. Jetton, & J. A. Dole (Eds.), *Adolescent literacy research and practice* (pp. 415–432). New York: Guilford Press.

Pressley, M., & Wharton-McDonald, R. (2002). The need for increased comprehension instruction. In M. Pressley (Ed.), *Reading instruction that works* (pp. 736–788). New York: Guilford Press.

Pressley, M., Wharton-McDonald, R., Raphael, L.M., Bogner, K., & Roehrig, A. (2002). Exemplary first grade teaching. In B.M. Taylor & P.D. Pearson (Eds.), *Teaching reading: Effective schools, accomplished teachers,* (pp. 73–88). Mahwah, NJ: Lawrence Erlbaum Associates.

Quiri, P. R. (1998). *Ellis Island.* New York: Children's Press.

Rasinski, T. V. (2003). *The fluent reader: Oral reading strategies for building word recognition, fluency, and comprehension.* New York: Scholastic.

Rasinski, T. V., Padak, N. D., McKeon, C. A., Wilfong, L. G., Friedauer, J. A., & Heim, P. (2005, September). Is reading fluency a key for successful high school reading?. *Journal of Adolescent & Adult Literacy, 49*, 22–27.

Reading a Food Label. (2007, November 19). *Scholastic News,* p. T3.

Samuels, S. J. (2002). Reading fluency: Its development and assessment. In A. E. Farstrup & S. J. Samuels (Eds.), *What research has to say about reading instruction,* (3rd ed., pp. 166–183). Newark: DE: International Reading Association.

Schraw, G. (2006). Knowledge structures and processes. In P. A. Alexander & P. H. Winne (Eds.), *Handbook of educational psychology.* Mahwah, NJ: Lawrence Erlbaum Associates.

Schwanenflugel, P. J., Meisinger, E. B., Wisenbaker, J. M., Kuhn, M. R., Strauss, G. P., & Morris, R. D. (2006, October/November/December). Becoming a fluent and automatic reader in the early elementary school years. *Reading Research Quarterly, 41*, 496–522.

Senge, P. M., Cambron McCabe, N. H., Lucas, T., Kleiner, A., Dutton, J., & Smith, B. (2000). *Schools that learn: A fifth discipline fieldbook for educators, parents, and everyone who cares about education.* New York: Doubleday.

Shanahan, C. (2004). Teaching science through literacy. In T. L. Jetton & J. A. Dole (Eds.), *Adolescent literacy research and practice,* (pp. 75–93). New York: Guilford Press.

Simpson, M. L., & Nist, S. L. (2002). Encouraging active reading at the college level. In C. C. Block & M. Pressley (Eds.), *Comprehension instruction: Research-based best practices* (pp. 351–364). New York: Guilford Press.

Sinatra, G. M., Brown, K. J., & Reynolds, R. E. (2002). Implications of cognitive resource allocation for comprehension strategies instruction. In C. C. Block & M. Pressley (Eds.), *Comprehension instruction: Researched-based best practices* (pp. 42–61). New York: Guilford Press.

Slater, W. H. (2004). Teaching English from a literacy perspective: The goal of high literacy for all students. In T. L. Jetton & J. A. Dole (Eds.), *Adolescent Literacy Research and Practice* (pp. 40–58). New York: Guilford Press.

Snow, C. E. (2003). Assessment of reading comprehension: Researchers and practitioners helping themselves and each other. In P. S. Sweet & C. E. Snow, (Eds.), *Rethinking Reading Comprehension* (pp. 192–206). New York: Guilford Press.

Sousa, D. A. (2006). *How the brain learns,* (3rd ed.) Thousand Oaks, CA: Corwin Press.

South Carolina Department of Education. 2007. *South Carolina academic standards for English language arts.* Columbia, SC: South Carolina Department of Education. Retrieved October 27, 2007, from http://ed.sc.gov/agency/offices/cso/standards/ela/documents/ELAStandards2007.doc.

Stahl, S. A. (2006). Understanding shifts in reading and its instruction. In K. A. Dougherty Stahl & M. C. McKenna (Eds.), *Reading research at work: Foundations of effective practices* (pp. 45–75). New York: Guilford Press.

Stahl, S. A., & Fairbanks, E. H. (2006). The "word factors": A problem for reading comprehension assessment. In K. A. Dougherty Stahl & M. C. McKenna (Eds.), *Reading research at work: Foundations of effective practice* (pp. 403–424). New York: Guilford Press.

Stahl, S. A., & Heubach, K. (2006). Fluency-oriented instruction. In K. A. Dougherty Stahl & M. C. McKenna (Eds.), *Reading research at work: Foundations of effective practice* (pp. 177–204). New York: Guilford Press.

Stahl, S. A., Jacobson, M. J., Davis, C. E., & Davis, R. L. (2006). Prior knowledge and difficult vocabulary in the comprehension of unfamiliar text. In K. A. Dougherty Stahl & M. C. McKenna (Eds.), *Reading research at work: Foundations of effective practice* (pp. 284–302). New York: Guilford Press.

Stahl, S. A., & Shanahan, C. (2004). Learning to think like a historian: Disciplinary knowledge through critical analysis of multiple documents. In T. L. Jetton & J. A. Dole (Eds.), *Adolescent Literacy Research and Practice* (pp. 94–118). New York: Guilford Press.

Stein, N., & Glenn, C. (1979). An analysis of story comprehension in elementary school children. In R. O. Freedle (Ed.), *Advances in discourse processing (Vol. 2)*. Norwood, NJ: Ablex.

Stille, D. R. (1999). *Wetlands, a true book.* New York: Children's Press.

Tierney, R. J. & Cunningham, J.W. (2002). Research on teaching reading comprehension. In R. Barr, M. L. Kamil & P. Mosenthal (Eds.), *Handbook of reading research* (pp. 609–656). Mahwah, NJ: Lawrence Erlbaum Associates.

Tovani, C. (2000). *I read it, but I don't get it: Comprehension strategies for adolescent readers.* Portland, ME: Stenhouse.

Trabasso, T., & Bouchard, E. (2002). Teaching readers how to comprehend text strategically. In C. C. Block & M. Pressley (Eds.), *Comprehension instruction: Researched-based best practices* (pp. 176–200). New York: Guilford Press.

Underwood, T., & Pearson, P. D. (2004). Teaching struggling adolescent readers to comprehend what they read. In T.L. Jetton & J. A. Dole (Eds.), *Adolescent Literacy Research and Practice* (pp. 135-161). New York: Guilford Press.

U. S. Department of Education, National Center for Education Statistics. (2007).*The condition of education, 2007.* (NCES 2007-064). Washington, DC: U.S. Government Printing Office.

Vacca, R. T. (2002). Making a difference in adolescents' school lives visible and invisible aspects of content area reading. In A. E. Farstrup & J. S. Samuels (Eds.), *What research has to say about reading instruction* (pp. 184–204). Newark, DE: International Reading Association.

VanSledright, B., & Limon, M. (2006). Learning and teaching social studies: A review of cognitive research in history and geography. In P. S. Alexander & P. H. Winne (Eds.), *Handbook of Educational Psychology* (pp. 545–570). Mahwah, NJ: Lawrence Erlbaum Associates.

Vellutino, F. R. (2003). Individual differences as sources of variability in reading comprehension in elementary school students. In A. P. Sweet and C. E. Snow (Eds.), *Reading Comprehension* (pp. 51–81). New York: Guilford Press.

Voices of Freedom (2007, February 5). *Scholastic Scope, 55*, pp. 14–15. Excerpted from Hampton, H. & Fayer, S. (1991). *Voices of Freedom: An Oral History of the Civil Rights Movement From the 1950s Through the 1980s.* New York: Bantam.

Walsh, K. (2004). *Our earth.* Huntington Beach, CA: Teacher Created Materials, Inc.

Whitcraft, M. (1999). *The Tigris and Euphrates Rivers.* New York: Franklin Watts.

Wiggins, G., & McTighe, J. (1998). *Understanding by design.* Alexandria, VA: Association for Supervision and Curriculum Development.

Williams, J. P. (2002). Reading comprehension strategies and teacher preparation. In A. E. Farstrup & J. S. Samuels (Eds.), *What research has to say about reading instruction* (pp. 243–260). Newark, DE: International Reading Association.

Wolfe, P. (2001). *Brain matters: Translating research into classroom practice.* Alexandria, VA: Association for Supervision and Curriculum Development.

Zull, J. E. (2002). *The art of changing the brain: Enriching the practice of teaching by exploring the biology of learning.* Sterling, VA: Stylus.

Index